EVIDENCE GROWTHGUIDE

The JOSH McDOWELL TRUTH-ALIVE SERIES

EVIDENCE GROWTHGUIDE

Part II

THE UNIQUENESS OF

THE BIBLE

By Josh McDowell
with Dale E. Bellis

Published by
HERE'S LIFE PUBLISHERS, INC.
San Bernardino, California 92402

EVIDENCE GROWTH GUIDE
PART II: The Uniqueness of the Bible

A Campus Crusade for Christ Book

Published by
HERE'S LIFE PUBLISHERS, INC.
P. O. Box 1576
San Bernardino, CA 92402

ISBN 0-86605-019-1
HLP Product No. 40-267-7
©Copyright 1982 by Campus Crusade for Christ

Printed in the United States of America

FOR MORE INFORMATION, WRITE:

L.I.F.E.—P. O. Box A399, Sydney South 2000, Australia
Campus Crusade for Christ of Canada—Box 368, Abbottsford, B.C., V25 4N9, Canada
Campus Crusade for Christ—103 Friar Street, Reading RGI IEP, Berkshire, England
Campus Crusade for Christ—28 Westmoreland St., Dublin 2, Ireland
Lay Institute for Evangelism—P. O. Box 8786, Auckland 3, New Zealand
Life Ministry—P. O. Box/Bus 91015, Auckland Park 2006, Republic of So. Africa
Campus Crusade for Christ Int'l.—Arrowhead Springs, San Bernardino, CA 92414, U.S.A.

Table of Contents

As You Begin

Why a Growth Guide?

Christians are challenged by their pastors and friends to read and study their Bibles, but many seem unable to maintain consistency. I've counseled hundreds of Christians who want to maximize their time in God's Word but struggle doing it. They know the Bible gives spiritual food, yet they are still hungry!

It is possible to transform your Bible study into Bible discovery. While this is not a book on Bible study methods, *Evidence Growth Guide, Part II* plunges you into practical Bible discovery. It directs your study by exploring fascinating aspects of God's Word. *Evidence Growth Guide, Part II* aids your journey, helping you to discover God's principles and to apply them to your life.

Barriers to Fruitful Study

There are numerous reasons we as believers fail to engage in firsthand contact with the Word. Intellectual arguments about the Bible's integrity and authority dilute our desire to know God's Word. Volumes of books have been written attacking the validity of the Scriptures. *Evidence Growth Guide, Part II* will equip you to evaluate what you hear and read about the Scriptures.

We often study the Bible and yet fail to recognize *why* and *what* we're studying. We get so engrossed in details we miss the main message. We lose sight of the forest because of the trees! *Evidence Growth Guide, Part II* will help you regain your perspective of the forest.

Many Christians are confused about the practical usefulness of the Scriptures in their daily lives. They doubt that the Bible relates to life in the 20th century. Consequently, this guide emphasizes application. As you approach each lesson, look for ways to translate what you learn into everyday terms. Share your insights with your friends, your family, or those in your study group. Sharing will solidify the practical benefits of each lesson.

God's One-of-a-Kind Communication

On his own, man cannot discover God (1 Corinthians 1:21). But God has not left us to ourselves. He has chosen to reveal Himself. In fact, God longs to tell us about Himself. He *wants* to be known.

God sovereignly chose to reveal Himself in a unique way. His acts of self-revelation occurred in history, especially through Jesus Christ, and Scripture preserves the accounts. The Bible is God's unique (one-of-a-kind) revelation of Himself to man.

If I am to know truth about God, I must find it in the Scriptures. God communicates to me in the words of Scripture. When I hold a Bible in my hand, I hold God's unique communication to man!

Not only that, but God speaks to me in the "language" of His Word. It is the only way I can know Him. That enhances the words of the Apostle Paul:

> How then shall they call upon Him in whom they have not believed? And how shall they believe in Him whom they have not heard? And how shall they hear without a preacher?
>
> So faith comes from hearing, and hearing by the word of Christ [Romans 10:14, 17].

Be Prepared to Explore

The lessons in this Growth Guide follow a specific format that will help you discover God's truth. The Growth Guide is self-contained, and the only other book or material you will need is your Bible. Every lesson contains key Scripture passages to guide you on your exploratory journey into God's Word. We recommend you use the New American Standard Bible.

Each lesson is divided into seven parts. Before you begin the first one, study the following thoroughly. You may also find it helpful to review this explanation as you begin the first few lessons. This will fix the parts more firmly in your mind.

A Quick Look Back

With the exception of Lesson One, each lesson begins with a review of the previous lesson. The language in these sections is personalized, to encourage you to apply the truths to your own life.

Key Truth

The primary truth dealt with in the lesson is crystallized, and the learning goals are clearly stated.

What Would You Say?

Interaction is the keystone of each lesson. Here you have an opportunity to stop, reflect, and reply to a common misconception expressed in conversational style. Consider the conversation to be personally addressed to you. How will you answer?

Let's Lay A Foundation

The core of each lesson consists of Bible study and basic instruction. Look up each Bible passage referred to and fill in the key words or analyze the passage for its meaning. As you progress through this part of your lesson, keep three major points in mind: (1) Consider. The questions sometimes draw from your present knowledge. Pause and respond to each of these opportunities. It will motivate you to search God's Word. (2) Contemplate. Each lesson is designed to maximize your interaction with God's Word. Allow the Holy Spirit to teach you as you analyze His truth. (3) Comprehend. Be certain you understand the main point before moving on. These lessons are like building blocks. If you miss one of the first blocks, it will be very difficult to fit the others properly into place.

Feedback

Here is an opportunity to test your comprehension. Without referring to the material you have just covered, try to complete this section. The exercises are both enjoyable and informative. If at the close there are areas you don't recall, don't hesitate to turn to that portion of the lesson and review.

My Response

Here we share together how God applies the truth to our lives personally. There are three parts: (1) I share how God has made a truth meaningful to me. (2) You are given an opportunity to consider what areas of your life God wants to affect with the same truth. (3) A specific prayer of application summarizes what we have just learned.

Identify with each expression and make it your own. Prayerfully consider how God can help you choose to make this true in your life.

For Further Reference

This section, included in most of the lessons, provides additional sources of information. It will give you the added advantage of reviewing the same material in different form. The books cited are available at your local Christian bookstore or can be obtained by contacting Here's Life Publishers, San Bernardino, CA 92402, (714) 886-7981.

What's Next?

Evidence Growth Guide, Part II is the second in a series of three growth guides. The first volume, *Part I: The Uniqueness of Christianity* may be studied in sequence or as a separate volume. Each guide is complete in itself.

Some might expect a study on the uniqueness of the Bible to be nothing more than a recitation of dry facts. Nothing could be further from the truth. The vitality of our faith relates directly to the evidence on which our faith is based. It is our goal to delve deeply into the reasons God's Word is the only reliable revelation of God to man.

The Bible instills right thinking. Right thinking shapes right living. And the Bible communicates God's standard for both.

Let's study together!

THE WORD

The Objective

In my back yard stands a bright red caboose. My kids love it! It took hard work and ingenuity to get it there. After three coats of paint, creative remodeling and a donated set of tracks, it serves as an attention-grabbing guest house. To me it symbolizes a spiritual truth.

Spiritual growth is like a train, and the Bible is the engine. God's Word teaches us about sin, Christ's provision, and man's destiny. But God is not content with merely feeding us information. He wants to bring us into fellowship with Himself and conform our behavior to His own. He wants to train us, not just teach us facts.

The word *training* comes from a Latin root that means "to pull along." When we allow the Word of God to train us, we permit it to pull us along like the engine of a train.

My caboose represents the conclusion of the "training" process, to be changed into Christ's likeness. Our objective in these studies is to permit God's Word to take us to our destination—knowing and being like Christ.

———————O———————

Key Truth

God's Word is designed to teach, reprove, correct and train believers.

I will learn:

- why the Bible alone is qualified to communicate God's view of life.
- four things God designed His Word to accomplish.
- the results God's Word will have in my life.

What Would You Say?

"You don't seriously believe that the Bible has any value to your life today, do you? It's an inspiring religious book, but don't take it too seriously. What does the Bible know about life in the 20th century? Raising a family? Staying financially solvent? Resolving emotional stress? It's a nice museum piece, but it can't help me today!"

What would *you* say?

I would say _____

_____

_____

Because _____

_____

_____

—————————————O—————————————

Let's Lay A Foundation

As we adventure through *Evidence Growth Guide, Part II*, we will discover why the Bible is the most dynamic book in history. To begin, let's examine three distinctive aspects of the Bible's uniqueness. This will lay a solid foundation for our study together.

I. The Bible possesses unique qualifications.

Christians agree that the Bible is a supernatural book. The Bible makes several unique claims about itself and its origin. No other book, religious or secular, possesses such qualifications as an authoritative communication from God.

1. Scripture is inspired.

The key Scripture passage on which *Evidence Growth Guide, Part II* is based is 2 Timothy 3:16-17. Take time to copy it out in full.

2 Timothy 3:16-17: _____

_____

_____

_____

"All scripture is inspired by God" is the clear declaration of Scripture concerning itself. Take a moment now to analyze your concept of inspiration. Compose a concise definition of inspiration.

Inspiration is_____

_____

_____

Our English word *inspiration* fails to describe Scripture accurately. It originates from two Latin words meaning "to breathe in." We speak of an "inspiring" poem or an "inspired" work of art because it fills us with emotion, ecstacy and wonder. The English *inspiration* means we receive an emotional or intellectual lift.

The Greek word translated "inspiration" means the very opposite. It is derived from two words meaning "breathed out by God." Scripture is God's breathed *out* words. The writers of Scripture aren't inspired; the writings are. The writers were aided by the Holy Spirit so that their words were also God's words. God, not the human writers, is the ultimate author of Scripture.

Inspiration means that God worked in a supernatural way to ensure that the words of the Scripture writers were the words of God.

2. Scripture is God's Word.

Thoughts are expressed in words, and Scripture claims that its words are the very words of God. They come from God and belong to God although expressed by human authors.

At the close of Moses' interview with God on Mt. Sinai, what does the Scripture say Moses recounted for the people (Exodus 24:3-4)? _____

_____

_____

Paul spoke with authority. Whose message did the Thessalonians receive and how did they accept it (1 Thessalonians 2:13)? _____

_____

_____

II. The Bible achieves a unique purpose.

This may revolutionize your view of God's Word! I encourage you to begin to expect God's Word to fulfill at least four functions in your life.

According to 2 Timothy 3:16, what four things is Scripture profitable for doing?

1.

2.

3.

4.

1. Inspired Scripture teaches me God's principles.

Much biblical doctrine is truth God has revealed about Himself. Scripture teaches me what God is like—His character, nature and attributes. His principles give me insight into His perspective on life. God's view is unlike my view. God sees all of life from an eternal perspective. My need is to see as He sees. Right thinking about God leads to harmony with God's principles.

2. Inspired Scripture reproves me of wrong.

Because all God's Word is truth, everything unaligned with it is false. Therefore, God's Word is as the final authority for determining right and wrong. God's Word exposes wrong thinking and living. It contrasts God's way with man's way and rebukes anything inconsistent with God's standard of life.

3. Inspired Scripture corrects my way.

Not only are we convicted of our wrong way, but we also are corrected and restored to God's way. God's Word gives positive steps for restoring us into harmony with God's principles of life. True harmony results as I align my thinking with God's.

4. Inspired Scripture trains me in right living.

Once having realigned my life into harmony with God, how do I continue to make that a part of my life? By taking God's training course in righteous living! I now learn the disciplines, taught to me by Scripture, for living godly. God's Word cultivates new habit patterns of behavior.

III. The Bible produces a unique result.

Second Timothy 3:17 completes our key passage. It reveals the result God's Word is to produce in our lives.

"All Scripture is inspired by God and profitable for teaching, for reproof, for correction, for training in righteousness; that the man of God may be

_____, _____ for every good work" (2 Timothy 3:16-17).

Two words help describe the Bible's results.

1. _____

Adequate means "complete, capable, efficient." Thus, the Scriptures provide everything to produce abundant, fulfilled living. God's Word makes our lives complete, capable of facing every test. What motivation to make God's Word a part of our lives!

2. _____

Scripture equips believers for effective, joyful living. We constantly need to be reinforced with God's power to resist the destructive forces of sin.

But there's something additional. Scripture equips us for "every good work," for a life-style that pleases God. God uses the Scriptures to outfit believers fully with the necessary skills for living in harmony with His principles of life.

Conclusion

God's purpose for His Word is achieved when we are adequately equipped— resourceful in facing life's crises and needs and fully outfitted for creative, abundant living. The Bible, God's inspired Word, is uniquely qualified to communicate God's view of life. It is His Word; it accomplishes His purpose and achieves specific results. That is summed up in Isaiah 55:11:

So shall my Word be which _____[origin];

It shall not return to me empty, without _____[purpose],

And without succeeding in the matter _____[result].

14

A summary of our study

The remaining part of our study divides into three sections. Each section relates to four ways Scripture achieves its purpose (teaching, reproof, correction, training). Each of these four functions directs us to the nature and character of God. However, no *one* function of the Scripture stands alone. Each works harmoniously and simultaneously with the others. There is a logical progression, divinely planned, to Scripture's design. Each function of Scripture depends on the other, operating in a cycle.

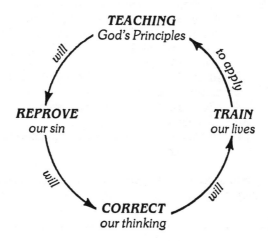

In Section 1, "The Unique Verification of the Bible," we will investigate evidence that verifies the supernatural characteristics of the Bible. In Section 2, "The Unique Purpose of the Bible," we will explore how the Scriptures teach, reprove, correct and train believers for abundant living. In Section 3, "The Unique Result of the Bible," we will discover the outcome of applying the principles of God's Word by examining the lives of four Old Testament characters.

In each section we will see something of what God is like. God's Word is supernatural because God is beyond the natural. Therefore, from the evidence of the supernatural character of the Bible (Section 1), to the purpose of Scripture (Section 2), to the results of God's Word in people's lives (Section 3), we will discover new insights into the character and nature of God. *Evidence Growth Guide, Part II* can be summarized in the following way:

THE UNIQUE VERIFI-CATION OF THE BIBLE Section 1	THE UNIQUE PUR-POSE OF THE BIBLE Section 2	THE UNIQUE RESULT OF THE BIBLE Section 3	THE NATURE OF GOD
The uniqueness of the Bible's continuity	The unique teaching of the Bible	Moses: Understanding God's righteousness	Righteous
The uniqueness of the Bible's influence	The unique reproof of the Bible	Jonah: Understanding God's judgement	Just
The uniqueness of the Bible's survival	The unique correction of the Bible	David: Understanding God's mercy	Merciful
The uniqueness of the Bible's circulation	The unique training of the Bible	Joseph: Under-standing God's power	All powerful

Without referring to the lesson, choose the correct answer to these multiple choice questions. Compare your answers with the key at the end of this lesson.

_____1. The Bible is uniquely qualified to speak God's mind because:
  A. All true Christians believe the Bible.
  B. The Bible claims divine authorship.
  C. No other religious book was written in Palestine.

_____2. The inspiration of the Bible means that:
  A. When I read the Bible I feel comforted.
  B. People receive creative ideas from the Bible.
  C. The words of Scripture have been breathed out by God while being written by men.

_____3. Based on 2 Timothy 3:16-17, what are some of the results God's Word will achieve in a believer's life?
  A. Reverses and setbacks will disappear.
  B. Wealth will replace poverty.
  C. Believer will be adequately equipped to face life's crises and skilled in right living.

Taking into account what you have learned in this lesson, how has your definition of inspiration changed?

_____

_____

_____

What four qualities in the character of God will this growth guide focus on?

1.

2.

3.

4.

—————————O—————————

My Response

Josh

It's exciting to share god's principles of life. I've realized, however, when I am sharing, I am not sharing my ideas, but God's. Scripture is the authority, not me! It's challenging to know that God never promised to bless what *I* said, but only what *He* said. That removes the pressure! My job is simply to give a mouth to the Scriptures. I realize that the convincing, teaching ministry of the Word is God's responsibility, not mine. I'm freed to share truth in the power of the Spirit without fear of failure. The results are in God's care!

_____

(My name)

What new truth has impressed me the most about God's Word?

_____

_____

_____

How will that make a difference in my life?

_____

_____

_____

To maximize the work of God's Word in my life, I will pray:

"Lord Jesus, cleanse my mind from distracting thoughts so You can speak to me through the Scriptures. Thank You for giving me Your Word to teach me Your truth, reprove my behavior, correct my faulty thinking and train me in Your ways. Make me alert to the opportunities that surround me to apply Your truth to my life. Amen"

———————O———————

For Further Reference

For a succinct analysis of the Bible's claims to inspiration, read Section I—"The Bible," in *Reasons Skeptics Should Consider Christianity*, pages 13-37.

KEY: B, C, C; Righteous, Just, Merciful, All powerful

Section 1

THE UNIQUE VERIFICATION
OF THE BIBLE

THE UNIQUENESS OF THE BIBLE'S CONTINUITY

A Quick Look Back

I have learned that the Bible is unique because it is a revelation of God's view of life. God communicates His perspective to me through Scripture in four ways: 1) He teaches me His principles; 2) He reproves me of wrong; 3) He corrects my responses to restore me to fellowship; and 4) He trains me in patterns of proper living.

———————O———————

Key Truth

The unique continuity of the Bible verifies its supernatural origin.

I will learn:

- how the differences among the authors of Scripture enhance the unity of the Bible.
- how the major theme of the Bible is preserved from beginning to end.
- how the Bible is unique from every other book in history.

What Would You Say?

"I've read parts of the Bible before, in college I think, and it didn't make sense to me. The problem is, there is no consistent message in the Bible, like in regular books. It's just a bunch of religious stories all written by different people, put together in a book with no logical connection. I guess somebody got the idea of collecting religious sayings and compiling them. I don't know why people spend so much time reading the Bible!"

What would *you* say?

I would say _____

_____

_____

Because _____

_____

_____

———————————O———————————

Let's Lay A Foundation

We will study in this lesson and the three lessons that follow, facts verifying the supernatural origin of the Bible. As believers, we accept the Bible as God's Word. But do we have any outside evidence that suggests that the Bible is a supernatural book? We certainly do! And studying facts verifying the supernatural character of the Bible will give you confidence in your personal witness. If, by this study, you are motivated to create additional opportunities for witness, we will have met our goal.

Remember, however, that no one fact about the Bible stands alone. Taken singly, the pieces of evidence are not conclusive. But taken together, these facts combine to demonstrate the uniqueness of the Bible as a revelation of God. On the whole, the evidence verifies the supernatural character of the Bible.

We will first examine the amazing continuity of the Bible. No other book equals the Bible in this characteristic. It is one book, yet many, a collection of writings. In fact, the word "bible" means "the books." But compared with other "bibles," this Bible is striking in its continuity.

To appreciate the Bible's continuity and unity, one must know something about its diversity. The Bible possesses great variety, yet it is one book.

I. Continuity through its development.

The Bible was written over a period of 1,500 years by more than forty authors and in circumstances which were highly diverse.

1. Written by a variety of authors from every walk of life.

Here is a sampling of biblical authors. Identify their different occupations.

AUTHOR	SCRIPTURE	OCCUPATION
Nehemiah	Nehemiah 1:11	_____
Amos	Amos 1:1	_____
Peter	Mark 1:16	_____
Matthew	Luke 5:27	_____

2. Written in a variety of places.

Identify the place where each of these men wrote.

AUTHOR	SCRIPTURE	PLACE
Ezekiel	Ezekiel 1:1	_____
Daniel	Daniel 7:1	_____
Paul	Ephesians 6:20	_____
John	Revelation 1:9	_____

3. Written during a variety of moods.

Identify the different moods in which this sampling of biblical authors composed their works.

AUTHOR	SCRIPTURE	MOOD
Jeremiah	Jeremiah 8:18, 21	_____
John	Revelation 1:17	_____
David	Psalm 103:1	_____
Solomon	Ecclesiastes 1:1-2	_____

4. Written under a variety of conditions.

What were the different conditions under which these men wrote?

AUTHOR	SCRIPTURE	CONDITION
David	1 Samuel 19:8	_____
Solomon	1 Kings 4:25, 30	_____
Jeremiah	Jeremiah 52:6	_____

God used each of those men, with their different viewpoints, abilities, conditioning and time periods, to record Scripture. What a diverse group! Yet when compared, each of their individual writings exhibits perfect harmony and continuity.

Not only was the Bible written by a variety of authors of differing occupation, mood, condition and place, but it was also written on three different continents—Asia, Africa and Europe. It was written in three different languages—Hebrew (most of the Old Testament), Aramaic (portions of Daniel) and Greek (all of the New Testament). Yet, when the books of the Bible are compared, they perfectly harmonize in theme and purpose. No other book, ancient or modern, has such credentials. This is one verification of its supernatural authorship.

II. Continuity of its theme.

The Bible's diversity is great. But in the midst of diversity there is unity. Each book of the Bible has an interdependent relationship with all the others. They depend upon one another. No one book tells the complete story.

Amazingly the Scripture writers wrote on controversial subjects, but totally without disagreement. The Bible addresses many religious, political and ethical subjects, yet exhibits perfect harmony from beginning to end.

So the Bible presents a complete story. God, man, sin, Satan, salvation and eternity are themes that run from Genesis through Revelation. What is introduced in Genesis is consummated in Revelation.

The parallels between Genesis and Revelation are more than coincidental. Complete the following comparison.

GENESIS	REVELATION
1:1 _____	21:1 _____
2:9-10 _____	22:1-2 _____
3:1 _____	20:10 _____
3:14-19 _____	21:4 _____

Paradise lost in Genesis is Paradise regained in Revelation. You cannot fully understand Revelation without understanding Genesis, nor Genesis without Romans, nor Romans without Leviticus, nor Leviticus without Hebrews. It is one continuous story of God's redemption of humanity through Jesus Christ. A Holy God extends salvation to sinful man, a miraculous plan of reconciliation.

Conclusion

It would be difficult to account for the amazing unity of the Bible by a natural explanation. The continuity of the Bible is unique and suggests a supernatural origin. No other book has such credentials.

The continuity of the Bible means:

- though written by a variety of authors, from different walks of life, in different places, during different moods, under separate conditions,

- the Bible possesses a common theme: God's redemption of man.

- an opportunity to witness to the Bible's supernatural and consistent message.

―――――――――O―――――――

Feedback

Without referring back to the lesson, answer these true/false statements. See the key at the end of the lesson for the answers.

True or false

_____1. There are many ancient books that match the Bible's unity of composition.

_____2. The biblical authors were so widely separated by time, culture and language that no amount of continuity can be discerned in their writings.

_____3. Over forty different authors were used of God to write the Scripture.

_____4. The Bible was written on three different continents (Asia, Africa, Europe), in three different languages (Hebrew, Aramaic, Greek).

_____5. The unity of the Bible is based upon the similarity of style, content and message of each book.

_____6. The Bible is a unified revelation of a righteous God desiring a relationship with man.

Consider this question:

From your own knowledge of Scripture, what do you consider to be the central message of the Bible?

_____

_____

_____

————————————O————————————

My Response

Josh

I was at the home of a close friend when a salesman for the *Great Books of the Western World* series came by. He spread out his literature on the *Great Books* and began his sales pitch. He became very interested when he learned we both lectured on university campuses. We could give him great contacts!

He spent five minutes talking with us about the *Great Books*. We spent an hour and a half talking to him about the greatest Book! I asked him, "If you took, not 40 authors, but just 10 authors; men from not different occupations, but from the same occupation; people from not different cultures, but from the same culture; authors writing not in different languages, but in the same language; writing not about many controversial subjects, but about just one controversial subject; what would you have?" He looked at me, back at the *Great Books*, and admitted, "A conglomeration."

Three days later he committed his life to Christ.

Any intelligent person, seeking for truth could acknowledge that the Bible's continuity is no accident. We cannot disregard its claims.

_____

(My name)

As a result of this study what new truth have I learned about God's Word that I never knew before?

_____

_____

_____

Knowing that the Bible is unique in its continuity of theme and message, discuss how understanding that would make excellent witnessing opportunities.

_____

_____

_____

To express my gratitude to God for His Word, I will make this prayer my own:

"Lord Jesus, I am struck with awe as I observe the beauty and perfection of Your Word. Your message of redemption and restoration beams through every book. I pray that You will open my eyes to see all the wonderful things contained in Your Word. I purpose to use this study as a time to know You better, as You reveal Yourself to me through Your Word. Amen."

————————O————————

For Further Reference

For a concise review of the uniqueness of the Bible in its continuity, read Chapter One of *Evidence That Demands a Verdict*, pages 15-17.

THE UNIQUENESS OF THE BIBLE'S INFLUENCE

A Quick Look Back

I have discovered that the unique continuity of the Bible helps verify its supernatural message. The Bible's continuity is truly astounding. Despite its variety of authorship and composition, Scripture presents one harmonious theme of God's redemption of man. No other book, ancient or modern, can boast of such qualifications. God's Word is unique in its continuity.

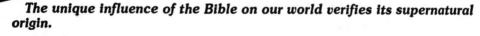

Key Truth

The unique influence of the Bible on our world verifies its supernatural origin.

I will learn:

- of the Bible's influence on literature.
- of the Bible's influence on law.
- of the Bible's influence on ethics.

What Would You Say?

"Religion—especially the Bible—produces a negative effect upon society. The Bible keeps a lot of ancient superstitions and religious myths alive. Fortunately, the Bible doesn't exert as much influence now as in the past. It's slipping. Primitive people were easily affected by prevailing religious notions. People today are more sophisticated."

What would *you* say?

I would say _____

_____

_____

Because _____

_____

_____

—————————O—————————

Let's Lay A Foundation

Our world is becoming more and more secularized. Several competent Christian leaders have written challenging books on the demise of Christianity in our Western world. Yet we still possess a rich heritage of biblical and Christian influences in our society. The Bible has permeated every level of society in an astonishing way.

I. The influence of the Bible on literature and speech.

1. Manuscript production.

   In ancient times, many of the techniques learned to preserve and produce manuscripts were learned as a result of transcribing the Scriptures which were constantly copied and re-copied.

   The art of transcribing primitive writings was an honorable profession. Many devoted their lives to it. King Hezekiah employed such a man. What

   were they called (2 Kings 18:18)? _____

2. Scrolls and books.

   Most ancient books were in the form of scrolls. Some scholars contend that the desire to study and preserve the Bible is responsible for the development of the book form we know today (technically called a codex) where sheets of paper are assembled in leaf form with writing on both sides.

3. Language.

   It's not surprising, because of the Bible's influence on literature, that patterns and figures of speech would also be influenced by the Bible.

   Isn't it curious how many Bible characters, illustrations, types and themes creep into common speech? Many colloquialisms originate from the Bible. See how many biblical cliches you can think of that have worked their way into popular speech. Match them to their biblical reference. Next time you hear one, take the opportunity to witness to the influence of the Bible!

FIGURE OF SPEECH	BIBLICAL REFERENCE
1. "The _____ of Job."	Job 13:15
2. "Older than _____."	Genesis 5:27
3. "Slower than _____."	Deuteronomy 29:2-5
4. _____	_____
5. _____	_____
6. _____	_____

II. The influence of the Bible on law and politics.

1. Law.

The similarities between modern law and Biblical legislation are stiking. Aspirations for justice, equality and legal protection of the innocent are shared by both the Bible and modern law. The different levels of punishment for different types of crime, as prescribed by Moses, are still active legal principles today. Note some of the features of Mosaic law that resemble modern legislation.

A. Regulations concerning manslaughter (read Exodus 21:12-14).

What foundational concept was established regarding the sacredness of life (vs. 12)?

_____

_____

_____

How much does a man's motive in a crime affect the sentence he receives (vs. 14)?

_____

_____

_____

B. The rights and responsibilities of property owners (read Exodus 21:28-36).

Under what conditions would a man's ox be killed (vs. 28)?

_____

_____

_____

What is necessary before the owner is responsible for his animal's behavior (vs. 29)?

_____

_____

_____

It should be noted that the familiar "Eye for an eye, tooth for a tooth" (Exodus 21:24-25) code of ethics was devised to *protect* an Israelite under the civil code. It provided equal punishment for an offense committed. No one was permitted to seek revenge or punish someone excessively.

2. Politics.

It may seem strange to some that the Bible has influenced politics. The Bible has been used to justify every conceivable form of government. Monarchy, democracy, capitalism, socialism, and even communism have all been argued from scriptural grounds.

Obviously the Bible has often been used incorrectly to support some of those positions. But whether the Bible has been used rightly or wrongly, the fact is that it has exerted a great influence on political theory. The Bible has been used to shape the great political issues of our time.

Based on your current knowledge, match the biblical passages that could be used to support the following political theories.

SCRIPTURE	THEORY	DEFINITION
1. Acts 4:32-35	a. Monarchy	Rule by a single person
2. Deuteronomy 17:14-17	b. Democracy	Rule by the majority
3. 1 Timothy 4:8	c. Communism	Property owned commonly by all
4. Acts 6:3-5	d. Socialism	State determines just and equal distribution of property and services.
5. Jeremiah 22:3	e. Capitalism	Ownership of private property

III. The influence of the Bible on ethics and philosophy.

One can hardly deal with ethics and philosophy without considering the Bible. It is difficult to find any system of ethics whose foundational principles are not already stated in the Bible. Philosophers always have struggled with the great questions of existence addressed by the Bible: Who am I? Why am I here? Where am I going? Many influential philosophical writers (Augustine, Aquinas and Pascal, for example) were Christians directly affected by biblical Christianity.

Ethical and philosophical truths from the Bible have thoroughly permeated our culture. Often popular sayings concerning human behavior can be traced to the Bible.

Complete the following list of popular sayings and see how many more you can list. Note how many have a biblical origin.

ETHICAL SAYING	BIBLICAL SOURCE OR BASIS
"An _____ for an _____, and a _____ for a _____."	Exodus 21:24
"Turn the _____ _____."	Matthew 5:39
"Spare the rod, _____ _____ _____."	Proverbs 22:15
_____	_____
_____	_____
_____	_____

Conclusion

The influence of the Bible on our culture and society is staggering. In literature, speech, law, politics, philosophy and ethics, the Bible's influence is clearly evident. Many individual books or writings have influenced our world in similar ways as the Bible, but not in the same scope and magnitude. Only the Bible exerts such widespread influence. This provides an open opportunity for believers to maximize their witness. In every level of society there is a residue of truth which can be used to make Christ an issue.

————————————O————————————

Feedback

Answer these questions without referring to the lesson. See the key at the end of the lesson for correct answers.

1. Name three main areas of our culture that have been influenced by the Bible

    (1)_____

    (2)_____

    (3)_____

2. What circumstance did the Mosaic law provide to limit punishment for taking a life?

    _____

    _____

    _____

3. Name at least three political theories that people have sought to advocate from the Bible.

    (1) _____

    (2) _____

    (3) _____

True or false

_____1. Other than on religious people, the Bible has had little influence on our society.

_____2. The type of influence the Bible has had on our society gives little opportunity to witness.

_____3. Many of the innovations in the production of ancient literature were spawned by the copying and reproduction of the Bible.

_____4. Nearly every ethical ideal stated in modern writings has already been stated in Scripture.

_____5. Our culture enjoys a rich heritage of biblical and Christian influences.

My Response

Josh

Before I became a Christian my knowledge of Scripture was very limited. That is why I could ridicule it—I had practically no personal knowledge of it. Yet, I did not realize the influence it had on my life through literature, law, ethics, and so on. After over 20 years of study and research I am still amazed at the powerful influence Scripture has had on history and our present world.

_____

(My name)

Following are some of the ways the influence of the Bible has affected my life prior to becoming a Christian.

_____

_____

_____

I will be alert to ways the Bible has influenced my world. The following are some opportunities I can use for witness.

_____

_____

_____

I will make this my prayer:

"Lord Jesus, I want to praise You for the powerful influence of Your Word in my life and in the world. Whatever justice and righteousness is evident in this world can be attributed to Your influence. I pray that You will help me to influence the society around me as I apply Your truth to my life. Amen."

Key: 1. Literature, law and ethics; 2. Equal punishment for an offense; 3. Monarchy, Democracy, Communism, Socialism, Capitalism.
1. False; 2. False; 3. True; 4. True; 5. True.

THE UNIQUENESS OF THE BIBLE'S SURVIVAL

A Quick Look Back

I've discovered how the Bible has permeated every level of society, exerting its influence on literature, law, politics, ethics and philosophy. God has given a witness of Himself in numerous places. All I need to do is take advantage of it. No other book in history has had such widespread influence. That adds to the evidence of the supernatural character of the Bible.

———————O———————

Key Truth

The Bible's survival through time, persecution, and criticism verifies its supernatural origin.

I will learn:

- how the Bible has survived through the centuries by careful copying and recopying.
- how the Bible has withstood the blasts of criticism.
- how the Bible has been validated as a book of history despite scholarly examination and criticism.

What Would You Say?

"Sure, I admit it! The Bible has been around a long time! That doesn't prove anything. It just shows that no one has challenged it. In the Middle Ages people had to agree with the Bible, or they got chopped! They were afraid to oppose it. People since have just blindly accepted the Bible because it's so old. That's the problem. No one has really examined the Bible to disprove it. When they do, it won't last long."

What would *you* say?

I would say _____

_____

_____

Because _____

_____

_____

Let's Lay A Foundation

When we hold a Bible in our hands, we're holding a book that's nearly 2,000 years old—parts of which are nearly 4,000 years old! The fact that the Bible has survived the centuries and come down to us intact is truly remarkable. Here, we will look at two features of the Bible's survival through the centuries and how that demonstrates that the Bible is a uniquely supernatural book.

I. Unique in survival through time.

No other book has survived the ravages of time like the Bible. Many misconceptions exist concerning the survival of ancient documents through the centuries. The questions in this lesson are designed to help you utilize this material in your practical witness. Answer each question based on your current knowledge or as one of your unbelieving friends would answer.

1. Before the invention of paper, what materials were used to write on?

_____

2. How much of our knowledge of historical events has come to us through handwritten manuscripts?

_____

3. How many manuscripts (handwritten copies) do we have to historically document Caesar's fighting the Gallic Wars?

_____

4. Do you know what ancient book has the second largest number of manuscripts surviving time and how many there are?

_____

5. Which ancient book has the largest number of manuscripts surviving time and how many are there?

_____

To understand why the Bible is unique in its survival through time, we must understand a little of the circumstances surrounding the printing of ancient literature. To preserve documents and literature before the development of the printing press (c. 1400), copyists, known as scribes, used utensils and materials much inferior to those of today.

The most common writing utensil was a reed pen, fashioned from rushes. Each scribe composed his own ink, mixing a special blend of charcoal, gum, water and other substances in a common pottery bowl. Other writing utensils included the chisel, used to engrave stones, and the stylus, used to make impressions on wax or clay tablets.

The materials on which the words of Scripture were transcribed were vastly different from our own day. Some of the most common forms of writing material included papyrus reed; parchment, made of leather strips; and tablets made of soft clay, which hardened into a permanent record.

Obviously, written records were constantly subject to decay, loss or defacement. Scribes were in the constant process of replacing worn and tattered copies with new ones. On and on the process would go, copying and re-copying the manuscripts, ensuring their use for later generations. This form of preserving history was the only technique used until approximately 550 years ago, when the printing press was invented.

The number of manuscripts of the New Testament alone that have come down to us is amazing. When you compare the number of surviving New Testament manuscripts with other works of antiquity the results are truly astounding. No other book in history has so many surviving manuscripts.

Rank the following ancient books according to the number of surviving manuscripts. Which is number one? Number two?

ANCIENT BOOK	NUMBER OF SURVIVING MANUSCRIPTS	COMPARATIVE RANK
Plato (Tetralogies)	7	#_____
Demosthenes	200	#_____
Caesar (Gallic Wars)	10	#_____
Tacitus (Annals)	20	#_____
Aristotle	49	#_____
New Testament	24,633	#_____
Sophocles	193	#_____
Homer (Iliad)	643	#_____

All that we know about Caesar and the Gallic Wars are from 10 manuscripts. When we compare that to over 24,000 surviving new Testament manuscripts, it gives us an insight into the Bible's amazing survival through time.

Now go back to the questions we began with and answer them based on the material you've just covered.

II. Unique in survival through persecution.

Imagine discussing these questions with an unbelieving friend. Answer them as you think he would.

1. How would Christianity benefit from destructive criticism of its enemies?

_____

_____

_____

2. What do you imagine would happen if an ancient empire officially decided to eliminate a popular manuscript from its realm?

_____

_____

_____

3. What open opposition and criticism has the Bible faced through the centuries?

_____

_____

_____

Throughout history there have been men who were devoted enemies of the Bible. Men have sought to destroy God's Word by burning and banning it. At times, kings, emperors, educators and philosophers all have attempted to put the Bible finally to rest—yet the corpse never stays put! No other book has withstood the vicious attacks of its enemies as the Bible.

Two examples illustrate how the Bible has resisted criticism and survived persecution. These are true ironies of history.

Example 1

In A.D. 303, the Roman Emperor Diocletion issued an edict banning Christians and their sacred book from the empire. In obedience to the edict, Roman soldiers went throughout the empire burning the Scriptures, destroying churches and executing Christians. Their hope was to free the empire from the hated curse of Christianity and the Bible.

But 25 years later, Constantine, the new emperor of Rome, became a Christian. He commissioned the historian Eusebius to prepare 50 perfect copies of the Scriptures for the government's library at the government's expense!

Example 2

Voltaire, the noted French skeptic and infidel, ridiculed the Bible and destroyed men's faith. He died in 1778. Prior to his death, Voltaire boasted that in one hundred years from his time, Christianity and the Bible would be swept from existence and pass into history

What has happened?

Voltaire has passed into history. Yet the irony is this: fifty years after Voltaire's death, the Geneva Bible Society moved into his house and used his printing press to produce thousands of Bibles to be distributed worldwide! Despite Voltaire's boast, the Bible continues to be loved by millions and studied by millions. *Voltaire* has passed into history; not the *Bible*!

A much more subtle attempt in destroying the Bible is to undermine the Bible's trustworthiness. If the credibility of the Bible as a true historical record is destroyed, everything taught by Christians is suspect.

Through destructive textual criticism, many modern theologians have regarded the teachings of Scripture as unhistorical and mythical. Many people's confidence in the Scriptures has been shaken because of the "assured results" of higher criticism. Never has a book been subjected to such intense scrutiny as the Bible. Every letter, word, line and precept has been scrupulously examined in search of reasons to doubt. By casting doubts on the Bible's integrity, critics have attempted to annul the Bible's influence through the "assured results of higher criticism."

And yet, I thank God for the critics!

Because of the critics, many keen minded, warmhearted Christian scholars have been even more encouraged to do their homework. Because of their research we can appreciate and trust the Scriptures all the more. These scholars have given a solid basis for our trust in the Scriptures.

Now return to the questions asked at the beginning of this point and answer each question based on what you've just read.

Conclusion

The Bible is unique in its survival through time, persecution and criticism. No other book in history has been subject to such scrutiny, critical analysis and hatred as the Bible. Yet it is still loved and read by millions. While skeptics and critics have predicted its demise, the Bible lives on as God's eternal Word. The survival of God's Word demonstrates that God *will* use His Word in spite of opposition.

———————O———————

Feedback

True or false

_____1. Scribes constantly recopied the Scriptures to replace decayed and worn manuscripts.

_____2. Parchment composed of strips of leather was a common form of ancient writing material.

_____3. Thankfully, the Bible has never been faced with severe persecution.

_____4. Modern critics of the Bible all agree the Bible is the authoritative Word of God.

_____5. No other ancient book has so many surviving manuscripts as the Bible.

———————O———————

My Response

Josh

I am humbled when I hold God's Word in my hand. When I think of the thousands of men who have devoted themsleves to the transmission of Scripture along with thousands of others who have given their lives for its propagation, I am encouraged. I praise God for His sovereign care over His Word and the committed servants of God who loved His Word.

_____

(My name)

Following is a list of discussion topics I now see as witnessing opportunities:

_____

_____

_____

The Bible being unique in survival tells me the following about God's character:

_____

_____

_____

I will share the following new insight with a friend as soon as possible:

_____

_____

_____

To better appreciate God's care of His Word. I will pray:

> *"Lord Jesus, I thank You that You have taken such care to place Your Word in my hand. I thank You for Your sovereign superintendence of Your Word. I understand that from its pages I learn more about Your greatness and character. Amen."*

———————O———————

For Further Reference

For a detailed explanation of the Bible's survival read *Evidence That Demands a Verdict*, pages 19-22.

For a fuller appreciation of how the Bible was prepared, read Chapter 2, "How Was the Bible Prepared," in *Evidence That Demands a Verdict*, pages 25-28.

KEY: 1. True; 2. True; 3. False; 4. False; 5. True.

THE UNIQUENESS OF THE BIBLE'S CIRCULATION

A Quick Look Back

I am amazed at how the Bible survives, even when faced by the severest opposition! I've learned that the Bible has survived the ravages of time, violent persecution and destructive criticism. It's survival is a supernatural verification that God *will* use His Word to make Himself known, despite the obstacles.

———————O———————

Key Truth

The Bible is unique in its circulation in the world.

I will learn:

- how the Bible outsells other books.
- about the Bible's amazing distribution.
- why the Bible is unique in its translation.

What Would You Say?

"So what! The Bible is an old book, it's been around for a long time, and if you look in the right place you can get hold of a copy. What does that prove? No one is interested in it anyway, especially intelligent people. The few Bibles that *do* get around are the product of a few Christian zealots in our country. Go outside our country and the Bible is practically non-existent."

What would *you* say?

I would say _____

_____

_____

Because _____

_____

_____

——————————O——————————

Let's Lay A Foundation

Did you ever try to keep a secret and no matter how careful you were, it just seemed to get out? Especially if the news is bad. "Press leaks" are a major problem to political administrations. No matter how sensitive the diplomatic issues or how critical the international negotiations, the word seems to get out.

God's Word is much like that! No matter how hard some have tried to suppress it, it still gets out. The circulation and spread of God's Word is truly amazing. In this lesson I want to share with you some facts about the Bible's circulation. I think it will help you understand the value of the Bible in your life.

We would expect that if the Bible is God's main communication to man, He will see to it that His book gets wide exposure. It is consistent with the nature of a supernatural God who longs to communicate personally through His Word with His creation, to distribute His Word more widely than any other book in history. That is exactly what we discover when we examine the evidence about the Bible. The vast circulation of the Bible is a verification of its supernatural origin.

Let's assume you are part of an official awards committee to select the most effective literature campaign of all time—the prestigious "Literature Circulation Award." You will be judging the campaign in three major categories: printing, sales, and translation.

Category 1 — Printing

Answer the following questions from your current knowledge. Return to them after reading the answers in the lesson material and make any changes you need to make.

1. What book, if the printed pages of all its copies were placed end to end, could carpet the globe?

_____

2. Since the invention of the modern printing press, what book has been printed and reprinted more than any other book?

_____

3. What book has the largest number of copies in print today? How many?

_____

The Bible and Bible portions have been in continuous print for over 4,000 years! Manuscripts have been laboriously hand printed, copied and re-copied, surviving the ravages of time and persecution. The first mechanical printing press, invented by Gutenberg, debuted by printing the Bible. Since Gutenberg, presses have churned out Bibles at an impressive rate, making it the most reprinted volume in history. The Bible has never been out of print!

The number of existing Bibles, both in manuscript form and print, is astounding. There are over 24,000 handwritten copies, and from the Bible societies alone, more than 2 billion 582 million Bibles, New Testaments, or individual Scripture portions have been printed. That's a lot of Bibles!

To understand how many Bibles that is, let's imagine that the task was given to one printer to produce over 2½ billion Bibles. To print every Bible, New Testament and individual Scripture portion published up to 1974, one printer would have to produce:

1 copy every 3 seconds
20 copies every minute
1,200 copies every hour
28,800 copies every day
10½ million copies every year
Non-stop
24 hours a day
For an amazing 245 years!

Category 2 — Sales

1. What book has sold more than any other, ever?

_____

2. What is the longest period of time most books retain their position as a best seller?

_____

3. In order to receive the coveted "Literature Circulation Award," what best-selling competition must the winner overcome?

_____

The Bible continues to be the number one best seller of all time. More Bibles have been sold, overall, than any other book in history. Some would argue that in any given month or year, more of a certain book was sold. And that is so. But no book has sustained the consistent number of sales the Bible has. The circulation and sales life of most books is extremely short, almost never more than a generation. No book has spanned the centuries, retaining its popularity, like the Bible.

That is all the more amazing when one considers the competition. To maintain a constant superiority of sales over all the other classics of history, both ancient and modern, is truly amazing. It must compete against ancient masters like Socrates, Plato, Aristotle, Homer and Thucydides. It must out-distance the classic literary giants, Chaucer, Shakespeare, Milton, Browning, Wadsworth and Poe. It must rise above the contemporary popularity of C.S. Lewis, J.R.R. Tolkien, James Michener and numerous other best selling authors whose works line our bookstore shelves. In addition, consider the stream of commentaries, sermons, Bible dictionaries, Bible encyclopedias, novels, theologies, biographies, church histories, lexicons, atlases and geographies sparked into existence by the Bible. Those are all books *about* the Bible, yet it outsells them all.

To think that the Bible must compete against the finest poetry, the most gripping novels, the most fascinating biographies and the most entertaining mysteries, and still be a best seller, is staggering. Matched against the greatest literature in history—the Bible outsells them all!

Category 3 — Translation

1. What book has had the greatest interest among all the cultures and nations of the world? To what degree?

   _____

2. To beat the nearest competition, into how many languages must the award-winning book be translated?

   _____

3. How many books are commonly re-translated to conform to changing language style?

   _____

One major factor accounting for the Bible's amazing circulation is its translations. No other book in history has been translated into so many different languages as the Bible.

Few books are ever translated into another language. Fewer yet are translated into multiple languages. Very seldom do you hear of a book's being translated into as many as 30 languages. To date, however, the Bible has been translated, in part or in whole, into more than 1,500 languages! The Bible is now available in the languages and dialects of 95 percent of the people of the world. On any given day, more than 3,000 people are working on Scripture translation. God has truly demonstrated His superintending power over the spread of His Word!

Even more astounding is the re-translation of the Bible. Did you ever consider that of the few books ever translated, fewer are re-translated to conform to modern language use? But the Bible is being re-translated constantly. There is a series of Bible translations and revisions in every major European language, and the English Bible has a lengthy history of re-translation. The number of these works is well over the thousand mark and several are added to the list each year.

Conclusion

It's time for a decision by the judges!

QUESTION: Does the Bible win the "Literature Circulation Award" as the most widely printed, purchased and translated book in history?

_____Yes   _____No

I vote yes! God has certainly demonstrated His power through the spread of His Word. The unique circulation of the Scripture suggests a supernatural guidance in its origin and distribution.

Without referring to the material you've just covered, how would you answer these statements?

1. Maybe the Bible *is* unique in its circulation. So what?

   _____

   _____

   _____

2. The Bible is not different from any other holy book. The Bible gets about as much exposure as other religious books do.

   _____

   _____

   _____

3. All the translations of the Bible that are available are confusing. Why do people keep turning out new translations?

   _____

   _____

   _____

—————————O—————————

My Response

Josh

The facts concerning the circulation of the Bible generate within me a profound respect for the men and women who love God's Word so as to distribute it worldwide. The spread of God's Word prepares the hearts of people to receive the gospel. I thank God for the sacrifice of men and women around the globe to get God's Word out. It causes me to want to be a better steward of the opportunities God gives me for witness, to be a part of the harvest.

_____

(My name)

How am I challenged through this study to be a tool in God's hands for spreading His Word?

_____

_____

_____

How can I use this truth in my practical witness?

_____

_____

_____

I will pray:

> *"Lord Jesus, I am thrilled when I understand that You are the one master-minding the spread of Your Word. Because it is so important to You, I purpose to make the study and application of Your Word to my life a major priority. Thank You for giving me the privilege of knowing You through Your Word! Amen."*

————————O————————

For Further Reference

For a concise review of the material in this lesson read *Evidence That Demands a Verdict*, pages 17-19.

For a usable answer to the question, "Which version of the Bible should I use?", read *Reasons Skeptics Should Consider Christianity*, pages 49-73.

Section 2

THE UNIQUE PURPOSE
OF THE BIBLE

THE UNIQUENESS OF THE BIBLE'S TEACHING

A Quick Look Back

I have come to realize that the Bible is the most circulated book in history! It holds the record as the most printed, sold, translated, re-translated and distributed book of all time. Through its widespread dispersion, God's power is demonstrated. He has communicated His standards of life and the way of fellowship with Him in every sphere of society. Because of the Bible's circulation, I have numerous opportunities to capitalize on the witness God has given concerning Himself.

———————O———————

Key Truth

God's Word reveals God's character by teaching me God's principles.

I will learn:

- that God's Word contains principles for life.
- that God's laws are an expression of God's character.
- that God wants obedience to be based on love.

What Would You Say?

"I really don't think it is necessary to live by all the rules and laws of the Bible. I don't see how they relate to me anyway. I live a good life. I'm kind to my neighbors and try to do a good deed when I can. I like to think I'm making this world a better place. That's the code I live by."

What would *you* say?

I would say _____

_____

_____

Because _____

_____

_____

———————————O———————————

Let's Lay A Foundation

The Christian life is an adventure in getting to know God. There are many ways to get to know a person. The best way is to know him as a friend, conversing in a casual way and listening to what he says about himself. The Bible is God's communication to man about Himself. We can't know anything for certain about God except what He has disclosed in the Scriptures. God shares with us what He is like, His likes and dislikes, through His laws. God's principles of life tell us about God's character.

I. God's Word instructs me in God's principles.

As a believer, I can be certain God has a plan for my life. He has charted that plan for me through certain principles of life. One major purpose for God's Word is to instruct me in God's principles. His principles are the guidelines I follow to find happiness and fulfillment in life. The more I discern and apply God's principles, the more I experience contentment and joy. I am happiest in life when I apply God's principles.

1. God's principles reveal God's ways.

God desires to acquaint us with His ways by teaching us His thoughts. The Bible is like a celestial window through which we see all of life as God sees it. I learn to think as God thinks by knowing God's book. God's thoughts about life take the form of principles expressed in His Word.

The book of Proverbs was written especially to instruct us in God's principles of life. Solomon explains in his preface that he wrote to instruct us in "wise behavior, righteousness, justice and equity" (Proverbs 1:3).

Solomon characterizes his instruction in the following way:

"Hear, O sons, the _____, and give attention that you may

_____, For I give you _____; Do not abandon my instruction" (Proverbs 4:1-2).

What will be the outcome of those who follow God's ways and observe His instruction?

"When I was a son to my father, tender and the only son in the sight of my

mother, Then he taught me and said to me, _____

_____; _____ "

(Proverbs 4:3-4).

48

"Hear my son, and accept my sayings, And the _____

_____" (Proverbs 4:10).

Solmon considers his words to be so important that he challenges us in four different ways to apply his instruction. Based on Proverbs 4:20, 21, what are four positive ways we can respond to God's principles of life?

1. "_____ to my words;"

2. "_____ to my sayings."

3. "Do not let them _____;"

4. "_____ in the _____."

2. God's principles light our way.

Learning how God thinks is not accomplished by natural means. Mental gymnastics and human logic won't help us here. As natural men, unable by natural means to discern God's way, we need the illumination of the Word.

Often in Scripture, God's principles are characterized as light, illuminating and pointing out the way. The book of Psalms frequently expresses this sentiment.

"The precepts of the Lord are right, rejoicing the heart; the commandment

of the Lord is pure, _____

_____" (Psalm 19:8).

The longest chapter in the Bible, Psalm 119, is devoted to extolling the virtues of the "law"—God's principles of life.

"O how I love Thy law! It is my meditation all the day. Thy command-

ments _____,

for they are ever mine. I have _____,

for Thy testimonies are my meditation. I _____

_____, because I have observed Thy precepts" (Psalm 119:97-100).

"From Thy precepts _____; therefore

I hate every false way. Thy Word is _____

_____, and_____

_____ " (Psalm 119:104-105).

II. God's principles reveal God's character.

I like to think of God's character, His principles and His laws like this:
God's *character* is the basis for His *principles* of life which produce His *laws*.
This might be visualized in a three-tiered way:

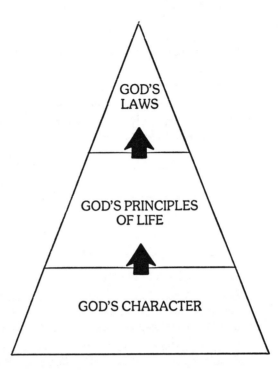

GOD'S
LAWS

GOD'S PRINCIPLES
OF LIFE

GOD'S CHARACTER

God expresses His character—and shows us how that character relates to our lives—in the framework of His principles. He then applies those principles to our lives in a practical way by His laws. God's laws were not arbitrarily established or created apart from Him; rather, they develop the principles which arise from His nature, His character.

As we have discovered, the Psalms abound with worship to God, telling what He is like. Psalm 19 praises God for what He is like by enumerating the characteristics of His law.

Analyze Psalm 19:7-9. What six words does David use to describe God's law?

1._____   4._____

2._____   5._____

3._____   6._____

What do these characteristics of the law tell us about the character of God?

_____

_____

_____

It is evident that all these things are true of God's Word because they are true of God. The key to understanding what God is like is to get personally acquainted with God through the Word. The Scripture reflects the qualities of its Author. This was the object in giving the law—to be acquainted with the lawgiver. Every law leads back to the knowledge and character of God.

Moses combines these two elements—keeping the law and fellowshipping with the lawgiver—in Deuteronomy 26:18.

"And the Lord has today declared you to _____

_____,

as He promised you, and that you should keep_____

_____."

Before God even gave His law through Moses what did He want the children of Israel to know above all else?

Exodus 6:7: _____

_____

_____

The phrase "know that I am the Lord" is used 14 times in Exodus. Keeping commandments is not an end in itself. Just following laws is not the object. That is the error of legalism. Obeying the law takes on significance only when we know God personally. Obedience is based on a love relationship with God.

Conclusion

God's Word is designed to teach me about the nature and character of God by explaining His principles. God's principles define His view of life. As I align myself with God's principles, I discover true fulfillment in life. Following laws, however, is not the object. The object of obedience is fellowship with God. His principles guide me to an understanding of His character.

———————O———————

Feedback

From your knowledge of the lesson, complete these summary statements. Refer to the key at the end of the lesson for answers.

1. God's Word _____ me in God's _____.

2. God's principles reveal _____ _____.

3. God's principles _____ our way.

4. _____ _____ reveal God's character.

5. God's Word _____ God's character by _____ me God's principles.

Josh

Rules and regulations can seem stifling. I've learned that God purposes that I follow His law on the basis of my love for Him and that I teach my children that they should obey God's law, not out of fear, but love. I express to Kelly, Sean and Katie that God's character lies behind every commandment and law. God's truth reveals what God is like. "Obey Christ," I tell them, "because you love Him and because of who He is." What freedom!

_____

(My name)

What new truth about Christ have I learned in this lesson?

_____

_____

_____

How has that changed my understanding of God?

_____

_____

_____

How does that apply to my life?

_____

_____

_____

In order to fix God's perspective in my mind, I will pray:

"Lord Jesus, thank You for Your Word that instructs me in Your ways. I purpose to follow You, not out of fear, but in love. I see that the solution to legalistic bondage is in loving You. Thank You for allowing me to know You better through Your Word. Amen."

For Further Reference

For an in-depth explanation of the attributes of God, read *Understanding the Cults*, pages 31-50.

KEY: 1. Instruct; principles; 2. God's way; 3. Illuminates; 4. God's principles; 5. Reveals; teaching

THE UNIQUENESS OF THE BIBLE'S REPROOF

A Quick Look Back

I have learned that one function of God's Word is to teach me what God is like by revealing God's standards for my life. Those standards take the form of principles that come from the very character and nature of God. Following God's ways, outlined in His principles of life, will bring me true joy and fulfillment in life.

————————O————————

Key Truth

God's Word reproves me when I stray from God's standards.

I will learn:

- the four purposes of God's law.
- the role the Holy Spirit has in reproof.
- the true motivation for obedience.

What Would You Say?

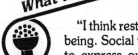

"I think restrictions that forbid certain conduct are extremely damaging to one's well-being. Social taboos originate from fear and are enforced by fear. We ought to be free to express ourselves and develop our own values. People don't need oppressive values forced on them."

What would *you* say?

I would say _____

_____

_____

Because _____

_____

_____

——————————O——————————

Let's Lay A Foundation

The word "law" is often used in Scripture to mean all God's standards of righteousness. Through the law, God makes clear the kind of God He is. When God gave His moral standards to Moses, Israel was terrified by God's greatness (Exodus 19:16). When they got close to Him they saw how unlike Him they were. That *is* a terrifying revelation! His standards are high!

The reproving ministry of God's Word is like that. The more I follow God's ways, the more I become acquainted with Him, which reveals how unlike Him I really am. My life is contrasted with God's standard for me.

The reproof of God's Word is a necessary ministry in our lives. The reproofs of Scripture explain where we have strayed from God's standards. Reproof helps us understand God's will for our lives.

I. The purpose of reproof.

Some would encourage us to believe that God's law has no value to our lives today. They possibly misunderstand the purpose of God's law. The reproving ministry of God's Word, expressed through God's law (standards of life), has a definite design and purpose.

1. To establish God's standards.

How is it possible for me to know God's standards? God's law makes God's standards clear. The law communicates what God expects.

"And now, Israel, what does the Lord your God require from you, but to

_____, to walk _____

and _____ and to

_____ with all your heart and with all your soul, and

to _____ and _____
which I am commanding you today for your good?" (Deuteronomy 10:12-13).

"He has _____;

And what does the Lord _____

But to _____, to _____,

And to _____?" (Micah 6:8).

2. To expose our condition.

Before we came to Christ, God saw us in our true condition, sinful and guilty. The problem was that *we* didn't know it! The law serves to awaken our conscience to right and wrong and show us our condition. The Bible reproves us of wrong by contrasting His ways with our ways.

Based on Romans 3:23, what is everyone's condition before God?

_____

_____

_____

According to Romans 3:20:

1) What is the law not able to do? _____

_____

2) What knowledge do we gain by the law? _____

_____

How did Paul say he came to know sin?

"What shall we say then? Is the law sin? May it never be! On the contrary, I

would not_____

except _____, for I

_____

if the _____"
(Romans 7:7).

3. To rebuke our sin.

The law never saves; it only condemns (Galatians 2:16). The law points out how sinful we are. When we try to obey the law in our own strength, we are helpless, condemned all the more. The reproof of God's Word goes beyond a rebuking slap on the wrist. It is a condemnation of death.

List key words from these passages in Romans that describe the reproving ministry of God's Word.

Romans 3:19 — "that...all the world may become _____ to God."

4:15 — "for the law brings about _____"

5:20 — "And the law came in that the _____ might increase;"

7:9 — "...the commandment came, sin became alive, and I

_____;"

7:10 — "...this commandment...proved to result in _____

_____ for me;"

8:2 — "...the law of...life...has set you free from the law of

_____ and of _____."

The law can never redeem us from our sin. It only increases the sense of sinfulness. It shows us there must be another way.

4. To lead us to Christ.

The law points us to the only solution of our sinfulness — faith in Christ. The law directs us to Christ as the only hope of fulfilling God's demands. The law so dramatically exposes our need, that we see Christ as the only one who can remove the penalty of death and the bondage of performance.

"For Christ is the _____ to everyone

_____" (Romans 10:4).

"Therefore the law has _____,

_____ that we may be justified by faith" (Galatians 3:24).

In Paul's day there was a household servant called the *paidagogos*. He was in charge of the child's moral welfare. His duty was to oversee the child's character development in preparation for manhood. One essential duty was to take the child to school each day. He was not the teacher, but was responsible to see that the child was under the teacher's care. This, Paul says, is like the function of the law. The law is to lead a man to Christ by showing him he is utterly unable to keep the law. Faith in Christ is the only hope of righteousness.

But didn't Christ also come to condemn us (John 3:17)?

_____

_____

_____

What did Christ redeem us from (Galatians 3:13)?

_____

_____

_____

As a believer, do I have any further responsibility to obey the law? If so, how can I fulfill it? Those questions, and many like them, have plagued Christians for centuries. The answer is found in my motivation for obeying Christ.

What key word keeps surfacing in these passages about obeying Christ?

Romans 13:8 _____   Galatians 5:6 _____

Romans 13:10_____   Galatians 5:14_____

Legalism is motivation by intimidation. Freedom is obeying Christ out of a motivation to please Him, in a word—*love*. If you want to remove the drudgery from obedience, fall in love with Jesus. Obeying principles is a *result* of our love relationship with Christ.

II. The person who reproves.

The Holy Spirit is the one that gives impact to the demands of the law. He quickens men's conscience and awakens them to sin. The Holy Spirit does not give a simple word of caution. He forcefully convicts the heart.

What does the Holy Spirit convict the world about?

"And He, [the Holy Spirit] when He comes, will convict the world con-

cerning _____ and _____ and

_____" (John 16:8).

Why does the Holy Spirit convict people about their sin (John 16:9)?

_____

Why does the Holy Spirit convict people about their need for righteousness (John 16:10)?

_____

Why does the Holy Spirit convict people about their impending judgment (John 16:11)?

_____

Conclusion

The Word of God reproves us of our sinful condition and improper living. Reproof gives us an understanding of God's standards by contrasting right and wrong. Most important, it points the way to Christ as the only solution.

A. What are four purposes of God's law?

1. _____

2. _____

3. _____

4. _____

B. What is the true motivation for obedience?

_____

_____

_____

C. How would you respond to the statement, "God's law has no value to our lives today"?

_____

_____

_____

_____

————————————O————————————

My Response

Josh

I've discovered that my relationship with my wife, Dottie, is similar to my relationship with Christ. My motivation to please Dottie grows out of my deep love for her. In spite of the areas of my life that need changing, Dottie still loves me. Her loving acceptance motivates me to be the kind of person I ought to be. A relationship of love motivates me to accept my wife's suggestions for change. Blind spots become a positive challenge to overcome, not a disheartening drudgery to endure. In the same way, I obey Christ, not because I *must*, but because I *want* to. I want to strengthen my love relationship with Him!

_____
(My name)

What new thought has occurred to me about the purpose of God's reproof?

_____

_____

_____

How will my sensitivity to God's reproofs aid me in my Christian walk?

_____

_____

_____

I purpose to respond to the reproofs of God's Word. What specific areas of my life has God used this lesson to reprove?

List them opposite God's standard.

MY LIFE	GOD'S STANDARD
1. e.g. exaggeration	e.g. Lay aside falsehood (Ephesians 4:25)
2.	
3.	
4.	

To reinforce my motivation to serve Christ out of love, I will pray:

"Lord Jesus, I thank You for the reproofs You provide me in Your Word. They are warning signals that keep me from walking in paths that would bring me pain and heartache. I understand Your reproofs to me to be motivated out of love. That causes me to want to please You all the more. Thank You for Your love. Amen."

———————O———————

For Further Reference

For a discussion of principles relating to love relationships, read *Givers, Takers and Other Kinds of Lovers*, pages 37-65.

The Uniqueness of the Bible's Correction

A Quick Look Back

I have discovered that God's Word has a ministry of reproof motivated out of love. It is this reproof that tells me what is right and wrong by contrasting God's righteous standards with my life. I have learned that while reproof exposes my condition and rebukes me, it also points to faith in Christ as the only solution.

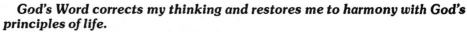

Key Truth

God's Word corrects my thinking and restores me to harmony with God's principles of life.

I will learn:

- that correction is to restore, not punish.
- the four steps to harmony with God's principles of life.
- how a renewed mind is essential for receiving correction.

What Would You Say?

"I admit that the Bible has had an influence on society even in the foundation for law and order. But, you can't expect the Bible to give an answer for every personal problem you have. Each person has solutions within himself. You need only to release the answers you already have. Our real problems will be corrected when we begin to realize our true self-potential."

What would *you* say?

I would say _____

_____

_____

Because _____

_____

_____

————————O————————

Let's Lay A Foundation

I. Correction requires renewal.

1. Renewal means a reinterpretation.

To accept correction requires a renewal of the mind. My *natural* response to correction is resistance! In order to welcome correction, a transformation must take place in the center of my thoughts. I must change the way I think. I must reinterpret all life's experiences in harmony with God's perspective.

I can't do that on my own. I need God's Spirit to change me by His Word.

Romans 12:2 succinctly sums up our need:

"And do not be conformed to this world, but _____

_____ by the _____

_____, that you may prove what the will of God is, that which is good and acceptable and perfect."

The renewal of our minds is based on a totally new category of thought. If we are to agree with God, we must think as God thinks. While every believer has received the Holy Spirit, all too often we fail to permit Him to renew our thoughts.

What has God given to every believer to know the thoughts of God (1 Corinthians 2:11,12)?

_____

_____

_____

As believers, what mind-set is necessary to interpret life accurately (Colossians 3:1,2)?

_____

_____

_____

2. Renewal means a new reality.

Often, God's reality is opposite ours. I've discovered that something is true with God only when it corresponds with God's facts. As reinterpreters, we must classify our experiences based on God's reality.

Transformed thinking doesn't happen overnight. We have years of human experience that has programmed natural thought patterns into our minds. Only through repeated application and practice do we begin to replace old thought patterns with new.

God's Word presents a reality that is opposite our own.

(1) We live through dying.

"Truly, truly, I say to you, unless a grain of wheat falls into the earth

and dies, it remains by itself alone; but _____,

_____ . He who _____

_____ , and he who _____

_____ in this world _____

_____" (John 12:24-25).

(2) We lead through serving.

"And He said to them, 'The kings of the Gentiles lord it over them; and those who have authority over them are called "benefactors." But

not so with you, but let him _____

become as _____, and the_____

as the _____'" (Luke 22:25-26).

(3) We exert power through weakness.

"And He has said to me, 'My grace is sufficient for you, for _____

_____,'

Most gladly, therefore, I will rather boast about _____

_____ , that the _____

_____ . Therefore I am well content with weaknesses, with insults, with distresses, with

persecutions, with difficulties for Christ's sake; for _____,

_____" (2 Corinthians 12:9-10).

II. Correction brings restoration.

Correction provides positive steps to restore us to harmony with God's ways. Correction shows me how to get back on track with God.

1. God's method of restoration.

God uses the familiar model of fathers disciplining their sons to illustrate His correction to us. Love is the motive behind God's correction. He demonstrates His fatherhood through His correction.

"My Son, do not reject the _____; or

loathe His reproof, for _____." Even as

_____" (Proverbs 3:11-12).

"Those _____, I _____

_____; be zealous therefore, and repent" (Revelation 3:19).

Often we mistake God's correction for punishment. Punishment focuses on past failure. Correction focuses on our progress in Christlikeness.

What is God's ultimate purpose for His correction (Hebrews 12:10)?

(1) "He disciplines us for _____."

(2) "That we may _____."

God's correction serves as a positive reminder of His love. Also, His corrections are His disciplines that lead to life. Though momentarily unpleasant, correction results in godliness and harmony.

"He whose ear _____ will

dwell among the wise. He who neglects discipline _____

_____ , But he who _____ acquires _____

_____" (Proverbs 15:31,32).

2. A personal strategy for restoration.

God's Word outlines the positive steps of correction that restore me to harmony with God's principles.

(1) Repent—recognize that the offense is against God.

King David committed adultery with Bethsheba and murdered her husband Uriah. Whom did David say he sinned against (Psalm 51:4)?

_____

Whom did Joseph say he would sin against if he committed adultery with Potiphar's wife (Genesis 39:8-9)?

_____

Repentance is an attitude that every believer should cultivate. It is the first and initial step to restoring harmony with God because, fundamentally, all sin is against God. Changing my attitude about my sin requires interpreting my offense as being, foremost, against God.

(2) Confess—admit the wrong.

An open confession to God regarding my wrong will confirm my change of attitude. Confession suggests an agreement with God. I acknowledge that my sin, which should be named specifically, is wrong and offensive to God. While this step intensifies the transformation of our minds, it is often a difficult one.

Why are people often unwilling to admit their sin (Proverbs 3:7)?

_____

_____

_____

When I truly confess my sin, I recognize that any attitude or action contrary to God's Word is wrong. On the basis of God's promise, I receive His forgiveness and cleansing by faith when I confess.

What does the person find who readily confesses His sin (Proverbs 28:13)?

_____

_____

_____

Confession, for the Christian, can be compared to breathing. Breathing requires two actions: exhaling and inhaling. Just as we exhale and inhale physically, so we can exhale and inhale spiritually. We exhale when we confess our sin. We inhale when we appropriate the fullness of God's Spirit by faith.

What has God promised the one who confesses his sin (1 John 1:9)?

_____

_____

_____

(3) Believe—trust God's evaluation.

Faith believes God's evaluation. Basic to faith is the recognition that our perspective is faulty but God's is true. Faith is simply believing and claiming as truth what Jesus Christ has said and done for us. Faith enables us to view ourselves as God views us—loved, forgiven and cleansed. Acknowledge His Word as true—even when it *appears* not to apply! He will make your way prosperous.

"Trust _____ with _____,

and do not _____,

In _____,
and he will make your paths straight" (Proverbs 3:5-6).

Faith claims in your own experience what God has already done for you through the death of His Son.

(4) Obey—practice your new perspective.

Obedience is the other side to the coin of faith. It is the natural response to believing God's evaluation as true. Obedience is faith in action.

"Who among you is wise and understanding? Let him _____

_____ in the gentleness of wisdom" (James 3:13).

In the practical experiences of life we have opportunity to learn obedience. As we pass through each experience, applying God's viewpoint and not our own, we cultivate patterns of obedience to God. That is precisely what Christ did.

"In the days of His flesh, when He offered up both prayers and supplication with loud crying and tears to Him who was able to save Him from death, and who was heard because of His piety, although He was

a Son, _____

_____; and having been made perfect, He became

_____ the source of eternal salvation; (Hebrews 5:7-9).

Conclusion

Restoration is the goal of correction, providing steps back to harmony with God's principles. As a prerequisite to following God's steps of restoration, we must have our minds transformed to think as God thinks. There are four positive steps of correction that reinforce this transformed thinking. 1) Repent—recognize the offense is against God; 2) Confess—admit the wrong; 3) Believe—trust God's evaluation; 4) Obey—practice our new perspective.

———————————O———————————

Feedback

What we consider true is often opposite to what God considers true. Match each Scripture reference to its corresponding statement of God's reality. See the key at the end of the lesson for the answers.

Matching:

1. 2 Corinthians 12:9-10		A. honor through humility
2. Proverbs 29:23		B. leadership through serving
3. Luke 9:48		C. life through death
4. Matthew 10:39		D. power through weakness

Agree or disagree (mark A or D)

_____1. The Holy Spirit is given to every believer to renew his thoughts to correspond with God's thoughts.

_____2. All committed Christians accept correction without resistance.

66

_____3. Punishment focuses on past failure. Correction focuses on our progress in Christlikeness.

_____4. Human evaluation is limited. I must believe God's Word in order to see and know accurately.

My Response

Josh

Recently, while eating supper with my family, I asked my six-year-old son, Sean, why he thought I had to discipline him. He told me "You have to, Daddy—you love me." I continued, "But why would I have to discipline you because I love you?" His answer crystalized the issue. "So we can play together, Daddy." Fellowship is the object of our heavenly Father's discipline. He shows me the way back into harmony with His Word.

_____

(My name)

What area of my thoughts is God seeking to renew?

_____

_____

_____

What specific circumstances is He using to get me to see as He sees?

_____

_____

_____

In order to grasp God's purpose for correction, I will pray:

"Lord Jesus, thank You for Your loving correction and discipline. You treat me as Your loving child. You are using life's circumstances to open my understanding to creatively apply Your steps of restoration. Right now I reaffirm my trust in Your viewpoint as eternally and unchangingly true. Amen."

For Further Reference

To better understand the believer's standing as a new sphere of reality, read "The Authority of the Believer," in *Understanding the Occult*, pages 196-202.

For further explanation of the concept of spiritual breathing, read *How to Experience God's Love and Forgiveness; How to be Filled with the Spirit;* and *How to Walk in the Spirit*, numbers 2, 3 and 4 in the *Transferable Concepts* series, by Bill Bright.

KEY: 1—D; 2—A; 3—B; 4—C

THE UNIQUENESS OF THE BIBLE'S TRAINING

A Quick Look Back

I've discovered that for me to profit from God's correction, I must have a renewed mind—one that evaluates life as God does. I have learned that correction will restore me to harmony with God as I follow the steps of repentance, confession, faith and obedience. I have seen this as a continuous process, one that aligns new areas of my life with God's ways.

————————O————————

Key Truth

Scripture trains me in patterns of godly living.

I will learn:

- that life's circumstances are the setting for training in righteousness.
- that faith in Christ is the key to proper living.
- that God has an individualized training program in righteousness for me.

What Would You Say?

"I think that each person is the master of his own destiny. Most of our problems are of our own making. Each person can create his own set of circumstances. If you're facing a tough situation you don't like, change it! You have the power to shape your own course in life. I believe when you give life your best, life will return its best."

What would *you* say?

I would say _____

_____

_____

_____

Because _____

_____

_____

_____

Of the four functions of Scripture, training completes the cycle. God's Word trains us in righteousness, making God's principles a way of life. This training is similar to what we do with our children. According to Proverbs 22:6, we are to train up a child in the way he should go. And again, in Ephesians 6:4, we are to raise children "in the discipline and instruction of the Lord." Training in righteousness directs the growth and development of godliness by practice and discipline.

I. Training in righteousness is through life's circumstances.

Training denotes a process. Training programs usually take place in a setting where certain skills can be developed by practice. So it is with God's training program for us.

1. Life's circumstances are the setting.

Our circumstances are always right. God so controls our environment as to place us in a setting uniquely suited for our needs. God knows precisely what we need to mold us into godly patterns of life. God uses the ordinary circumstances of life to work for our ultimate good—being made like Jesus Christ.

This is the meaning of God's righteousness. Whatever God does is right; His actions are always consistent with His character. What God *is* determines what God *does*. God does everything right!

So rest assured, God will not place us in a circumstance of life that is unproductive of our progress in righteousness. He so controls our development in Christlikeness that He is able to bring into our lives the very things we need to train us in godly behavior.

"And we know that _____

_____ to those who love God, to those who are _____

_____" (Romans 8:28).

How did Paul respond to the different circumstances God placed him in (Philippians 4:11-12)?

_____

_____

_____

What are we to do under similar circumstances? What will we ultimately receive (James 1:12)?

_____

_____

_____

70

2. Application is the objective.

The reason life is the setting for training in righteousness is that life is where righteousness is to be applied. God desires that I learn how to apply His truth to my life. Application promotes true understanding. Understanding is the ability to discern how truth applies to life.

The most popular phrase in Proverbs is: "The fear of the Lord is the beginning of wisdom." Yet, how is "understanding" developed (Proverbs 9:10)?

_____

_____

_____

A sound knowledge of what God is like is necessary for discerning how truth applies to me. When I know what is true about God, I can clearly see what is *not* true of me.

Will just a mental knowledge of God's principles ensure my keeping them (Psalm 119:34)?

_____

_____

_____

The old adage, "practice makes perfect," may have some truth to it! Applying God's truth to our lives is done by practice. The mature person has discerned how to apply God's truth to life consistently.

"For every one who partakes only of milk _____

_____ , for he is a babe. But solid

food is for _____ , who _____

_____ to _____

_____" (Hebrews 5:14).

II. Training in righteousness is by faith.

God desires that we grow in Him by the training process of trusting Him completely. He never allows situations to come our way for the reason of tempting us.

"Let no man say when he is tempted _____

_____; for God cannot be tempted by evil and _____

_____" (James 1:13).

71

If God is not tempting me to sin, are trying circumstances a test of my character? According to James 1:2-3 when we encounter trials, what is being tested and what does it produce?

_____

_____

_____

It is impossible to apply God's principles to life without faith. Mere human effort is ineffective. We have a deadly enemy that works against us in practicing righteous behavior—sin. But by faith we resist our old habit patterns, affirm that we are dead to each one (Romans 6:6) and begin the process of cultivating new patterns of righteousness. That is the value of tests. Each test gives us a crisis opportunity to accept God's view of life and reject our own. As we've discovered, training in righteousness requires a whole new orientation to life. Yet faith trusts God's Word rather than human reasoning.

Where does Paul say righteousness comes from and on what basis (Philippians 3:9)?

_____

_____

_____

Difficult circumstances give us an opportunity to exercise our faith in God, resulting in righteousness, praise and honor to God. A response of faith to testing circumstances trains us in godly responses to life.

"In this you greatly rejoice, even though now _____

_____ , you have been distressed _____

_____ that the _____

_____ , being more precious than gold which is

perishable, _____ may be found

_____ at the

revelation of Jesus Christ" (1 Peter 1:6-7).

Conclusion

Of the four functions of Scripture in each believer's life, training in righteousness completes the cycle. Training makes God's principles a way of life. There are two ways God makes His principles a consistent part of our lives. The first provides the setting. The second, the means. *Life's circumstances* are the setting for training in righteousness; *faith* is the means by which we receive righteousness. Trials and testing circumstances of life provide an opportunity to exercise faith in God. My response of faith trains me in godly responses to life. God causes each situation to be especially fitted for me.

Without referring to the material you have just covered, show that you have learned how life's circumstances train us in righteousness by completing these sentences. Check your answers with the key at the close of this lesson.

1. God causes each of life's circumstances to work together for our _____.

2. We are in life's training program so that truth can be_____ to our lives.

3. Righteousness is applied in our lives on the basis of _____.

4. Trying circumstances are a test of our faith, not a test of our _____.

True or false

_____1. God tempts us to sin to determine whether we are strong.

_____2. Trials are opportunities to try harder to live a righteous life.

_____3. Trials and tests are opportunities to place my faith in God who has promised to provide for me and protect me.

_____4. God will not place us in a circumstance of life that is unproductive of our progress in righteous living.

—————————O—————————

Josh

When faced by trying circumstances or temptation, I used to ask, "Lord what lesson is in this for me? What area of my character do You wish to build?" I soon learned that was the wrong question to ask. Whenever I am confronted with a difficult trial now, I ask, "Lord, what are You attempting to teach me about yourself? What aspect of Your nature do You wish me to trust?" I find myself in repeated circumstances when my faith is being tested. It is particularly trying when people miss a deadline or they fail to follow through with details. There are times when my plane is late and it adversely affects my entire speaking schedule. As these frustrating circumstances test my faith, I am reminded that God is in complete control. He knows my situation. He cares and has definite plans to accomplish His sovereign will through me. He wants me to trust Him. Those circumstances are times when my faith in Him as the controller of my life is being tested. I thank Him for those tests, because my faith is stronger. I am learning to respond much more swiftly to irritations in life in a manner honoring Christ.

_____

(My name)

What particular truth, clear to me in theory, do I find difficult to apply in practice?

_____

_____

_____

What circumstance in my life do I see God giving me the opportunity to trust Him? How can I apply the truth of this lesson to my life today?

_____

_____

_____

I will make this prayer my own:

> *"Lord Jesus, I thank You for the training You are putting me through. It is my opportunity to learn how Your righteous ways are to be applied to my everyday living. Help me to trust You when my faith is being tested. Amen"*

Section 3

THE UNIQUE RESULT
OF THE BIBLE

MOSES: UNDERSTANDING GOD'S RIGHTEOUSNESS

A Quick Look Back

I have learned that God's Word fulfills at least four functions in every believer's life. Scripture teaches God's principles, reproves departures from God's standards, corrects wrong thinking, and trains in godly patterns of life. The result of God's Word fulfilling those four roles in a believer's life is profound. Believers are adequately prepared in facing life's crises and equipped to live abundant, fulfilled lives.

———————O———————

Key Truth

Through the life of Moses, the righteousness of God is revealed.

I will learn:

- that God's law is righteous because God is righteous.
- that God wants us to obey His law from the heart.
- how the law gives us insight into God's nature.

What Would You Say?

"I do my best to live as I should. God knows that we are human and that we'll fail. He doesn't expect us to be perfect. I think at the end of life God will just weigh my good deeds against my bad deeds; and if my good deeds outweigh my bad deeds, I'll be rewarded. I just plan to live the best I can."

What would *you* say?

I would say _____

_____

_____

Because _____

_____

_____

––––––––––––––––O––––––––––––––––

Let's Lay A Foundation

God used Moses to make His Word known to the children of Israel and consequently to us. As we study the life of Moses, the lawgiver, I think we will discover one undeniable fact: there is a personal, righteous God behind each law. God revealed Himself to Moses as a person who desires a relationship with man.

Although God is truly righteous, He does not desire just a legal adherence to a set of rules. The law was given in the context of God's revealing the way of fellowship with Him. Ultimately, God longs to have personal fellowship with each of us.

I. The law is from a righteous God.

God did not disclose everything about Himself at one time. God progressively revealed Himself through a series of events, each one disclosing more of what He is like. Progressive revelation continued until God was fully revealed in His Son. In Jesus Christ, God is fully unveiled. In Him, the invisible God is made visible (Colossians 1:15). Yet to Moses, God unfolded his plan for fellowship in stages. He introduced himself to Moses by first explaining His name.

1. The authority of His name.

In Exodus 3, God appeared to Moses in a burning bush, explaining how He planned to relieve the oppression of His people. When God commissioned Moses to lead Israel out of Egypt, Moses felt inadequate. To help Moses convince Israel that Moses was genuinely sent of God, He told Moses His name.

"And God said to Moses, _____; and He said,

thus you shall say to the sons of Israel, _____

_____" (Exodus 3:14).

In Old Testament times names were significant. A name described the person. When God said, "I am that I am," He described something about Himself. His name, as given to Moses, describes His self-sufficiency. He does not *need* anything or anybody in order to be complete. He is complete in Himself. Nothing exists outside of God necessary to make God God. God alone, because of His character, is self-sufficient. "I am that I am" reveals the self-existent self-sufficiency of God.

God being complete in Himself, chose to fellowship with man. He didn't *need* to; He *chose* to.

God initiated His relationship with Israel through Abraham. When God made His promise to Abraham in Genesis 22:16 to make of his family a great nation, through whom the whole world would be blessed, God sealed His promise with an oath. He swore by His own name. Since God's name represents His self-sufficiency, he could swear by nothing greater! God's name cannot be compared. No higher authority exists than God. He is who He is—the absolute God.

2. The righteousness of His name.

God's introduction to Moses was not just a revelation of His absolute power and authority. It was also a revelation of His character. God is Holy.

"Do not come near here; remove your sandals from your feet, for the place

_____ "
(Exodus 3:5).

The reverence Moses had for God was probably, at first, out of fear. But God made Moses know that more than spectacular fireworks was involved. God is Holy. And that was the message God instructed Moses to give His people. In fact, all the laws God gave Moses were given to teach Israel (and us) God's righteousness.

"Speak to all the congregation of the sons of Israel and say to them,

_____ for

_____ " (Leviticus 19:2).

Briefly, glance over the rest of Leviticus 19. What follows God's charge to

be holy?_____

_____

The word *holiness* is an abstract term, hard to visualize. How do you think God was to teach His people (and us) the meaning of holiness?

_____

Through the law, God taught the meaning of holiness. He legislated many external ceremonies and requirements for Israel. The ceremonies were important, not in themselves, but in what they illustrated. Each was an object lesson visualizing separation from defilement and sin, and separation to God. Israel would never have understood holiness unless it were illustrated in familiar terms.

The psalmist praised God for the Holiness of God's name:

"Let them praise Thy _____; _____

_____. And the strength of the King_____

_____; Thou has established equity (uprightness);

Thou hast_____

_____ in Jacob. Exalt the Lord our God, and worship at His foot-

stool; _____ "
(Psalm 99:3-5).

79

II. The law is from a personal God.

All God's laws are pathways constructed for the purpose of knowing Him. He desires that His law, His way, be a part of building a personal relationship with Him.

1. God desires a relationship.

What special relationship did Israel have with God (Deuteronomy 7:6)?

_____

_____

_____

Why did God choose Israel, not someone else (Deuteronomy 7:7-8)?

_____

_____

_____

How do God's laws provide the way for a loving relationship with God (Deuteronomy 7:9)?

_____

_____

_____

Moses understood God's desire to have a personal relationship better than anyone. Exodus 33:11 says God would speak to Moses "face-to-face, just as a man speaks to his friend." Moses understood the purpose of teaching God's ways. He knew that the law would teach him to know God, and, by knowing God be able to please Him.

"Now therefore, I pray thee, if I have_____

_____ , let me _____

_____ that I _____,

_____ in thy sight"
(Exodus 33:13).

2. A relationship produces obedience.

God desires that obedience to the law be a *result* of a love relationship, not a basis to produce one. God does not want mere performance. Duty produces obligation, not joyful obedience.

"Behold, Thou dost desire truth_____

_____.

Thou wilt make me know wisdom" (Psalm 51:6).

"For Thou_____

80

_____, otherwise I would give it; Thou _____

_____ . The

sacrifices of God are _____

_____,_____

_____ "

(Psalm 51:16-17).

What kind of service were the children of Israel giving God (Isaiah 29:13)?

_____

_____

_____

Why was their performance not pleasing to God (Isaiah 29:13)?

_____

_____

_____

Based on Psalm 40:6-8:

What does God not desire?

_____

_____

_____

What attitude must I have in order to obey God genuinely?

_____

_____

_____

Conclusion

The law was given to Moses, first, so that God's people would know God's character. God is righteous. God initially revealed the meaning of righteousness through His name. He illustrated the meaning of righteousness by legislating external ceremonies and requirements. Each ceremony was an object lesson defining holiness—separation from defilement and sin. Second, God gave His law to prescribe the way for a personal love relationship with Him. Obedience and right living become a natural by-product of that love relationship.

Multiple Choice.

Without referring to the lesson, answer these multiple choice questions.

_____1. My obedience to God's law should be because:
   A. I am committed to the law.
   B. I am committed to love God with my whole heart.
   C. I am committed to my responsibility to obey.

_____2. The law is fundamentally good because:
   A. It comes from the righteous nature of God.
   B. It protects our society from evildoers.
   C. It shows me how to live a good life.

_____3. The fundamental purpose for learning God's law is to:
   A. Gain insight on how I am to live.
   B. Gain insight into God's nature.
   C. Gain insight into my character.

_____4. When someone violates God's principles it primarily indicates:
   A. They don't know God's principles exist.
   B. They aren't committed to obeying God's law.
   C. They aren't in love with the lawgiver.

_____5. God's ultimate purpose in revealing Himself through His Word is to:
   A. Provide social standards for proper living.
   B. Provide a plan to restore men to a personal relationship with God.
   C. Provide a reason to condemn men.

Completion

Fill in the missing words in these sentences.

1. God's law is righteous because God is _____.

2. Duty produces _____, not joyful obedience.

3. God's name, as given to Moses, describes His _____.

4. All of the laws God gave Moses were given to teach us God's _____
   _____.

5. All of God's laws are pathways constructed for the purpose of _____
   _____.

———————O———————

Josh

The foundation to knowing the reasons I believe is found in the proper understanding of God's law. Behind every one of God's laws are principles that speak of His righteous nature. Before I became a Christian, I examined the evidences for Christianity. I came face-to-face with Christ's claims to be God. Unable to refute those claims intellectually, I trusted Christ as Savior and Lord. The "whys" of my faith were based on my conviction and understanding that Christ was who He said He was—the Son of God. My continual growth is also based on my conviction and understanding of who God is. By learning His ways I obtain a growing insight to who He is—His nature—His character. I have found in order to know more of why I believe I must trace the reason for God's ways back to His character.

_____

(My name)

What new insight into God's character have I discovered from this?

_____

_____

_____

What impact will that have on my relationship with God?

_____

_____

_____

To affirm my understanding of God's law, I will pray:

"*Lord Jesus, You are the great "I Am"—the personal God behind each law given. Thank You for giving me Your laws so that I can know You. Focus my attention, not on Your laws, but on my relationship with You. Thank You for providing a way to know You personally. Amen.*"

KEY: Multiple Choice: B, A, B, C, B.
Completion: 1. Righteous, 2. Obligation, 3. Self-sufficiency, 4. Righteousness, 5. Knowing God.

JONAH: UNDERSTANDING GOD'S JUDGMENT

A Quick Look Back

I have discovered that God desired a personal relationship even in the Old Testament. God gave His law to help us comprehend His personal holiness. God's law relates to the personal nature of God. I've also learned that righteousness and acceptance with God are not based on obedience to the law. Righteousness comes only by faith in Christ. My obedience to Christ is a *result* of my love relationship. God wants His people to obey Him out of love, not to gain acceptance, but to develop a relationship.

———————O———————

Key Truth

Through the life of Jonah the judgment of God is proclaimed.

I will learn:

- that proclaiming God's reproofs is a necessary ministry.
- how accepting God's reproof is the first step toward correction.
- how rejecting God's reproof brings judgment.

What Would You Say?

"A God of judgment and wrath would have to be a tyrant. I just don't believe God is like that. He loves His creation. He is patient and kind and will not reject people for minor infractions. I think the only hell and judgment we face is the hell and judgment we bring on ourselves."

What would *you* say?

I would say _____

_____

_____

Because _____

_____

_____

————————————◯————————————

Proclaiming God's reproofs is a necessary part of the ministry of God's Word in our lives. It was the distinctive ministry of the Old Testament prophets to proclaim God's reproofs. They warned the people of judgment if they did not obey God. The promise of judgment effectively deters evil.

Jonah was a prophet with a message of reproof. His message caused people to fear God and repent. The Book of Jonah has a dual plot: the story of the prophet Jonah, and God's reproof of a city, Ninevah. This lesson illustrates, through the life of Jonah, the reproving ministry of God's Word. It demonstrates that God always judges sin, and His judgments are always just.

I. God judges disobedience.

I've sometimes said, "God may be your Father, but He's not your dad!" God is often caricatured as a doting grandfather, weak-willed and permissive, smilingly excusing the sins of His children. People who think of God that way fail to account for all that God's Word says He is like. God is love, yet His love is coupled with His justice. God's justice demands that sin be punished. Thankfully, God's justice is tempered by His mercy. And likewise, His mercy is balanced by His righteousness. No one attribute of God supercedes the others. Each attribute is held in perfect balance.

So God is both a God of love and judgment. With God, judgment is always the consequence of sin. God is holy and just, and He cannot excuse evil. He is a God of judgment who reproves and convicts unrighteousness. While it is true that God is love, the other side of love is judgment. If God is holy, there must be judgment.

What did God tell Jonah to do (Jonah 1:1-2)?

_____

_____

_____

What was God's evaluation of Ninevah (Jonah 1:1-2)?

_____

_____

_____

What was Jonah's response to God's commission (Jonah 1:3)?

_____

_____

_____

How did God reprove Jonah of his disobedience?

Phase 1 (Jonah 1:4): _____

_____

_____

Phase 2 (Jonah 1:15): _____

_____

_____

Phase 3 (Jonah 1:17): _____

_____

_____

II. God's judgment is just.

When God reproves us, how do we know that God is just in His evaluation?

1. God searches our hearts.

"I, the Lord, _____, I _____

_____, even to give to each man

_____, according to the

_____" (Jeremiah 17:10).

2. God knows our motives.

"For the Word of God is _____ and _____

and _____ than any two-edged sword, and _____

_____ as far as the _____ of _____,

of both _____, and able to_____

_____of the heart" (Hebrews 4:12).

3. God judges righteously.

"The fear of the Lord is clean, enduring forever; the _____ of

the Lord are _____; they are _____" (Psalm 19:9).

III. God's judgment depends on our response.

The consequence of rejecting God's reproofs is judgment. But the purpose of God's judgment is to warn, offering a way of escape. God warns us through the reproofs of His Word. It is because of His mercy that He reproves and warns us. It is because of His love that He provides salvation, an escape from the consequences of sin.

Rejecting reproof has its consequences; accepting reproof has its rewards.

Rejecting reproof:

"They would _____

_____, they spurned _____

_____. So they shall _____

_____

_____, and be satisfied with _____

_____

_____" (Proverbs 1:30-31).

Accepting reproof:

"But he who _____

_____, and

shall be at ease _____

_____" (Proverbs 1:33).

Reproofs and "enjoying" the fruit of our rebellion can become the first steps toward correction. This was true of Jonah.

Where did Jonah's rebellion, and God's reproof, put Jonah? What did it cause him to do (Jonah 2:1)?

_____

_____

_____

Through Jonah's prayer, we get an inside look into what God taught Jonah about Himself. Jonah learned how intolerant God is of sin and rebellion. Jonah discovered that God gives a just reward to those who rebel against His authority. Equally, God rewards those who repent and believe.

What did God's reproof cause Jonah to choose to do (Jonah 2:9)?

_____

_____

_____

When did Jonah choose to obey God? What did God do (Jonah 2:10)?

_____

_____

_____

Following Jonah's reproof, what was his response when God commissioned him the second time to preach to Ninevah (Jonah 3:2-3)?

_____

_____

_____

God never changes. His opinion toward sin has always been the same: judgment. He has an everlasting hatred of sin. However, He lovingly accepts those who change *their* minds about sin and believe His Word. The reason God was going to destroy Ninevah was their wickedness.

How did the people of Ninevah respond to Jonah's message of judgment (Jonah 3:5)?

_____

_____

_____

It's true. God doesn't change. Only people change. The people of Ninevah changed in their attitude toward God and their sin. Ninevah repented because the people believed Jonah's message of judgment.

What was God's response to Ninevah's faith and obedience (Jonah 3:10)?

_____

_____

_____

The reason God did not destroy Ninevah was that the people changed their minds about their sin. Jonah was unhappy with the revival that struck Ninevah. He had wanted to see the city destroyed (4:3). But God gave Jonah an object lesson. He caused a plant to grow and to shade Jonah while he waited on the hillside to see what would happen to the city. God caused that same plant to die by sending a worm to kill it. Jonah was displeased.

What did God's object lesson teach Jonah about God's attitude toward those who want to turn from evil (Jonah 4:11)?

_____

_____

_____

Conclusion

God's justice is demonstrated through His reproofs. God is just in His attitude toward sin and sinners and toward those who repent and believe. God is a God of mercy, but He is also a God of judgment. Judgment comes based upon our decision to respond to God's reproof and believe, or reject God's reproof and rebel. His reproofs warn us of judgment to follow.

———————O———————

Completion

Without referring to the material you have just covered, try to complete the following sentences. Check your answers with the key at the close of this lesson.

1. God was going to destroy Ninevah because of their _____.

2. Ninevah repented because they believed Jonah's message of _____ _____.

3. The reason God did not destroy Ninevah was that the people _____ _____ about their sin.

4. God's justice demands that sin _____.

5. There are three ways we know that God's judgments are just: God searches our _____, God knows our _____ and God judges _____.

Agree or disagree (mark A or D)

_____1. God always judges sin, and His judgments are always just.

_____2. God never changes in His attitude toward sin. He forgives those who seek forgiveness and judges those who rebel.

_____3. The more I understand God's hatred for sin the more I understand His love for sinners.

_____4. Once God decides to bring judgment on a person or nation nothing can change his mind.

My Response

Josh

I maintain a very heavy travel schedule, on the road sometimes 20 days out of a month. I've discovered that it is hard for me to say no to requests to speak, but I need to! My family suffers when I get over-committed.

The best way for me to keep a balance between ministry and family is to make myself accountable to others. I have given permission to a few close friends to confront me when they sense I'm not giving adequate time to my family. And they do it! Recently a close friend challenged me about my schedule, urging me to cancel some speaking engagements in order to spend quality time with my family. Canceling those meetings was the hardest thing I can remember doing in my ministry. But it was worth it! I thank God for faithful friends who reprove me with God's Word when I stray from God's best for my life.

_____

(My name)

In what area of my life is the Holy Spirit reproving me?

_____

_____

_____

I will respond to His reproof in the following way:

_____

_____

_____

What consequences of sin have I avoided because of my obedience to the reproofs of the Spirit?

_____

_____

_____

In gratitude for the reproofs of God's Word, I will pray:

> *"Lord Jesus, Your judgments are true and Your reproofs righteous. I thank You that You love me enough to warn me of the destructiveness of sin. I praise You that You made a way to escape the judgment of sin by giving Yourself as ransom for my sin. Amen."*

———————O———————

KEY: Completion : 1. Wickedness; 2. Judgment; 3. Changed their minds; 4. Be punished. 5. Hearts, motives, righteously.

DAVID: UNDERSTANDING GOD'S MERCY

A Quick Look Back

I have learned that God's reproofs are an important ministry to my life. As was shown by Jonah and the people of Ninevah, heeding reproof is the first step to restoration with God.

―――――――○―――――――

Key Truth

Through the life of David the mercy of God is established.

I will learn:

- that all my sins first originate from an inner response against God.
- how faith in God prevents sin.
- that obedience to God's principles is a result of faith.

What Would You Say?

"I think there's just not enough love in the world. We need to love ourselves and our fellow men. If we are ever to solve the problems of war, hunger and poverty, it will be because we have learned to accept people the way they are. Every person has the capacity to care. Deep within each person is a reservoir of human compassion—we need only to unleash it to solve the problems of the world."

What would *you* say?

I would say _____

_____

_____

Because _____

_____

_____

———————————O———————————

Let's Lay A Foundation

When we stray from God's way, God's Word puts us back on track. That describes the correcting ministry of God's Word in our lives. The Word gives us positive steps to restore us to harmony with God's principles. Because God loves us, He has a wonderful plan for our lives. And we cannot realize the full potential of God's plan for us when we are out of harmony with Him. That is why God has given us corrective steps to restoration.

This lesson corresponds with our previous study on the correcting ministry of God's Word. In this lesson, we will discover how King David violated the teaching of God's principles, was reproved of his sin, and took the corrective steps to restoration. The story of David's sin is chronicled in 2 Samuel 12. In David's life we are able to see both the mercy of God and the destructive consequences of sin. Even though David was restored to fellowship with God, the consequences of sin did not stop. Sin is always costly. God immediately forgave David, yet sin took its toll in David's life.

The steps King David took concerning his sin illustrate how we are to respond to the correcting ministry of God's Word in our lives.

I. Recognize the offense is against God (repent).

What was King David's inner response against God that resulted in his outward response to others? Read 2 Samuel 12:1-15 and respond to the following:

Who confronted David with his sin (vs. 1, 7)? _____

By defining "despised" (vs. 9) describe David's inner response to God.

_____

_____

_____

What outward offenses did David commit as a result of his wrong response to God (vs. 9)?

_____

_____

_____

94

What were some of the destructive consequences resulting from David's sin (vss. 10, 11)?

_____

_____

_____

Whom did David believe he had truly sinned against? Uriah? Bathsheba (vs. 13)? _____

David reiterated this truth in his prayer of confession.

"Against _____, _____, I have

_____, and done_____

_____, so that _____ when

thou dost speak, and blameless when _____

_____" (Psalm 51:4).

II. Admit the sin to God (confess).

Once David was confronted with his offenses he did not hide them. He quickly confessed his sin. God responded to David's contrite heart and honored his ready confession.

"Then David said to Nathan, 'I have sinned against the Lord.' And Nathan

said to David, 'The Lord also has _____

_____; you _____'" (2 Samuel 12:13).

In Psalm 32 David readily acknowledges the benefits of confessing our sin to God and the disadvantage of attempting to hide our sin.

The joy of confessed sin:

"How _____ whose _____,

whose _____

_____. How _____ to whom the Lord does not impute iniquity, and in whose spirit there is no deceit!" (Psalm 32:1-2).

The consequence of unconfessed sin:

"When I kept silent about my sin, _____

_____ through _____. For

day and night Thy hand _____; my

vitality _____ as with the fever heat of summer" (Psalm 32:3-4).

The recommended solution:

"I _____ to thee and my iniquity _____

_____; I said _____

_____ my transgression to the Lord; and thou didst

_____ the guilt (iniquity) of my sin" (Psalm 32:5).

III. Trust in God to provide (believe).

David's sin against God originated in his lack of faith. David did not trust God to meet his needs. He did not consider God able to provide for him.

The apostle Paul, in analyzing the cause of sin in a believer's life, said:

"The _____ which you have, have as _____

_____. Happy is he who does not condemn himself in

what he approves. But he who doubts is condemned if he eats, because his

eating is not _____; and whatever_____

_____" (Romans 14:22-23).

How had God provided for David in the past? Would God have done more (2 Samuel 12:7-8)?

_____

_____

_____

David's essential sin was refusing to trust God's timetable for meeting his needs. God was anxious to provide for David, yet David chose to provide for his own needs instead of trusting in God. By refusing to submit to God's authority, David took matters into his own hands, not believing that God knew best how to provide for him. When *we* determine where and when God's provisions are acceptable, we deny our faith in God as the only one capable and knowledgeable enough to meet all our needs.

Later, David learned that faith, trusting God as provider, was essential to a restored, happy life. He purposed to allow God to meet all his needs. The songs of David record praises to God as faithful provider.

"Delight yourself in the Lord; and He will _____

_____. Commit your way

to the Lord, _____

_____" (Psalm 37:4-5).

IV. Practice the principles of God (obey).

When David recognized his sin as against God and confessed and trusted in God as provider, his faith resulted in obedience. Obeying the law of God became a natural by-product of his faith.

David discovered that in order to lead a joyful, abundant life, he needed to be continually informed of God's standards for this life. Obedience came as he applied God's principles to life. Obedience is nothing more than faith in action.

What did David discover would keep him in harmony with God (Psalm 119:11)? _____

_____

David poses a practical question and answers it.

"How can a young man keep his way pure? By keeping it _____

_____ . With all my heart

_____;

Do not let me wonder _____

_____ "

(Psalm 119:9-10).

Conclusion

Our outward response toward others is governed by our inward response toward God. God will respond to our faith by forgiving us and meeting all our needs. That is why faith is all important in our relationship with God. Faith submits to God's timetable in meeting our needs and opts to practice God's principles, even when it's not convenient.

———————O———————

Feedback

Agree or disagree (mark A or D)

_____1. My faith response toward God is caused by my outward response toward others.

_____2. My sinful offenses toward others are caused by my lack of faith toward God.

_____3. A sin such as adultery is a direct sin against God.

_____4. Living by faith in God as supplier of all my needs would prevent adultery.

_____5. God intends my faith to result in obedience to His principles of life.

My Response

Josh

As a young Christian I struggled to balance my understanding of God's love for me and His expectations of me. I knew He loved me even though I failed. Yet I knew He wanted me to obey His laws. This struggle was resolved as I focused on my inner response to God. I soon realized it was my faith He was ultimately concerned with. As I grew by faith in Him, proper performance followed.

_____

(My name)

In what specific area of my life do I sense God wants to provide for me?

_____

_____

What sin can I avoid as I choose to allow God to provide for me?

_____

_____

_____

What area of temptation will I face if I fail to allow God to provide for me?

_____

_____

_____

To submit to God as my ultimate Provider, I will pray:

"Lord Jesus, I thank You for Your merciful provisions for every area of my life. I submit to Your control, knowing You know how best to supply my needs. When I fail, You tenderly convict me of my sin and show me positive steps to restoration. Help me to strengthen my faith relationship with You by trusting Your provisions daily. I purpose to follow Your principles of life out of love, not obligation. Thank You for the correction of Your Word. Amen."

JOSEPH: UNDERSTANDING GOD'S POWER

A Quick Look Back

I have understood that faith is essential in my relationship with Christ. Rather than moving prematurely ahead to satisfy my own needs, I will trust in God's provisions no matter how long the delay. I have learned that my outward response to others is a direct result of my inward response to God. Obedience is a *result* of my faith, putting in practice what I believe God says is true.

———————○———————

Key Truth

Through the life of Joseph the power of God is demonstrated.

I will learn:

- that God wants to use everyday circumstances for my good and His glory.
- how difficulties can be transformed into opportunities for growth.
- that God has a purpose for my life and controls my destiny.

What Would You Say?

"My philosophy is that problems will always be with us, so just don't let them get you down. Life is like sailing; when the wind blows, ride it out. Believe me, what comes will come, you can't prevent it. The main thing is don't allow difficulties to affect your happiness. We can't change what happens, so be happy in spite of circumstances."

What would *you* say?

I would say _____

_____

_____

Because _____

_____

_____

—————————O—————————

It is in the everyday experiences and circumstances of life that God wishes to train us in righteousness. The experience of Joseph is an ideal example of how God uses trying circumstances to train a man for righteous living. This lesson illustrates through the life of Joseph the training ministry of God's Word. We will discover how Joseph was adequately equipped through life's experiences for God's service.

Difficult circumstances may be considered from two vantage points—God's and man's. From the human viewpoint, Joseph's sufferings were due to the jealousy of his brothers, the injustice of Potiphar and the ingratitude of the butler. From God's viewpoint those years were for the purpose of training Joseph in righteousness. Joseph had repeated opportunities to apply God's principles to life. His training in servanthood equipped him for his great leadership role as Pharoah's right-hand man. If we look from a human perspective, we become discouraged with what happened to Joseph. However, God wants us to understand circumstances as He sees them—as opportunities to apply His principles of life.

I. Purpose through circumstances.

God caused every circumstance to work for Joseph's good and God's glory. Nothing came into Joseph's life that God did not use to accomplish His divine purpose. Joseph came to believe: "that God causes all things to work together for good to those who love God, to those who are called according to His purpose" (Romans 8:28).

God's purpose is not always immediately clear. As Joseph accepted each circumstance as an opportunity to serve his Master, God's purpose unfolded.

What circumstances of Joseph's life did God use for His own purpose and design? Skim through the story of Joseph and complete these key verses. Joseph's story is recorded in Genesis 37-50.

1. "When they saw him from a distance and before he came close to them,

they _____

_____ " (Genesis 37:18).

2. So it came about when Joseph reached his brothers, that _____

_____ , the

varicolored tunic that was on him; and they took him and _____

_____ . Now the pit was empty without any water in it"
(Genesis 37:23-24).

3. "Then some Midianite traders passed by, so they _____

   _____, and _____

   _____ for_____

   _____ . Thus they _____

   _____" (Genesis 37:28).

4. "Now Joseph had been taken down to Egypt; and Potiphar, an Egyptian

   officer of Pharoah, the captain of the bodyguard,_____

   _____ who had taken him down there" (Genesis 39:1).

5. "So Joseph's master took him and _____, the

   place where the _____

   _____; and he was there_____"
   (Genesis 39:20).

6. "Then Pharoah sent and called for Joseph, and they hurriedly _____

   _____. And when he had shaved himself and

   changed his clothes, he _____" (Genesis 41:14).

7. "And Pharoah said to Joseph, ' _____

   _____'" (Genesis 41:41).

II. Training in circumstances.

All of Joseph's experiences and circumstances had been designed for his training. If Joseph had viewed his situation from a human standpoint, depression would have been his constant companion. Everything was against him. But he recognized that these very experiences, (slavery, imprisonment, and so on) were the ones God wished to use to train him. God controls our circumstances; we don't. Trying circumstances only give us an opportunity to respond in faith to God. Trusting Him is the way to transform difficulties into opportunities for growth.

How did Joseph respond in each circumstance? What were the results in Joseph's character?

1. With Potiphar.

   "And _____, so he became a _____.
   And he was in the house of his master the Egyptian" (Genesis 39:2).

2. In jail.

   "The chief jailer did not supervise anything under Joseph's charge

   because_____

   _____; and whatever he did, _____"
   (Genesis 39:23).

101

Who did Joseph believe sent him to Egypt? Who gave him his leadership position?

"Now, therefore, it was not _____, but _____; and _____

_____ and _____ and _____" (Genesis 45:8).

Glancing back through history, we are able to see how Joseph was used to accomplish God's work. Saved from the ravages of famine, Joseph's fledgling family was nurtured into a mighty nation, through whom came the Redeemer. Joseph was given a strategic role in fulfilling God's purposes. Joseph believed God could use any circumstance, no matter how difficult, for God's ultimate glory and Joseph's personal good.

"And as for you, _____, but _____

_____ in order to bring about _____

_____, to _____"
(Genesis 50:20).

As Joseph was dying at the age of 110, how did he demonstrate his confidence in God's ability to control circumstances (Genesis 50:24, 25)?

_____

_____

_____

Conclusion

Joseph's response of faith to God transformed his bewildering circumstances into opportunities for growth. Joseph's training in godly responses to life's circumstances was conducted without warning. Yet, because Joseph trusted God, he gained rich insight into God's purposes for his family, and eventually the redemption of mankind. God uses trying circumstances to train us in righteous patterns of life. God is sovereign and is causing each circumstance to work to the eventual good of each of us who walk by faith.

———————————O———————————

Feedback

From your knowledge of Joseph's story and this lesson, answer these true/false statements. See the key at the end of the lesson for correct answers.

True or false

_____1. God gave advance knowledge of all that would happen to Joseph and the reasons those things would take place.

_____2. God was in complete control of each circumstance of Joseph and was training him in righteousness.

_____3. Pharaoh chose Joseph as leader because he had run an effective advertising campaign and had previously been mayor of a city.

_____4. Joseph was trained at the University of Egypt majoring in management and dream interpretation.

_____5. When Joseph looked to his past he could see God's controlling hand on his life.

————————O————————

My Response

Josh

When I joined Campus Crusade for Christ over 19 years ago, my ambition was to be a traveling youth speaker. When I would not cooperate with an unauthorized policy that I knew Dr. Bright was opposed to, a few in leadership positions found a way to remove me from the scene. Unknown to Dr. Bright, they assigned me to Argentina. I was tempted to "fight" this assignment by going to Dr. Bright with the problem. Instead I felt restrained and remembered the need to submit in order to learn leadership through servanthood. As a result my two years in Latin America were precisely what I needed. The experience equipped me with skills in university debates and the free-speech lectures. After God had sufficiently prepared me in spirit and mind, Dr. Bright learned of my situation. Dr. Bright immediately called me out of "exile." From that call my university lecture ministry was born. While a few misguided men meant to remove me, God meant to prepare me. God is in control!

_____

(My name)

What difficult circumstance have I had recently that God could be using?

_____

_____

_____

_____

_____

As a result of my circumstances how will I respond?

_____

_____

_____

_____

Training in righteousness takes place in life's circumstances. I will reaffirm my trust in God's control and pray:

> *"Thank You Lord Jesus for the present circumstances I am in. Help me to see my trials as opportunities to trust You. You are all-knowing and have my best interest at heart. I thank You for Your loving kindness and sovereign control. Amen."*

––––––––––––––––O––––––––––––––––

For Further Reference

(For more examples of God's control of circumstances, read pages 79-82 and 123-141 of *Josh, The Excitement of the Unexpected*, written by Joe Musser and published by Here's Life Publishers, San Bernardino, California, ©1981.)

NOTES

NOTES

107

NOTES